COLLINS

Kitchen
GARDEN

ANDI CLEVELY

HarperCollins*Publishers*
London

HarperCollins*Publishers*
London

First published in 1999 by HarperCollins*Publishers*

Design and layout © HarperCollins*Publishers* 1999
Text: © Andi Clevely 1999

A catalogue record for this book is available
from the British Library.

ISBN 0-00-414107-5

Designed and produced for HarperCollins*Publishers* by
Cooling Brown, Middlesex, England
Editorial: Carole McGlynn, Ann Kay
Design: Arthur Brown, Alistair Plumb, Tish Mills, Pauline Clarke
Photography: Peter Anderson, Steve Gorton

For HarperCollins*Publishers*
Editorial Director: Polly Powell
Managing Editor: Becky Humphries
Production Manager: David Lennox

Colour origination: Colourscan

Printed and bound in Great Britain by Scotprint

Contents

Introduction 4

Designing a Kitchen Garden 6

The Ornamental Kitchen Garden 8

Developing a Productive Garden 10

Digging and Cultivation 12

Planning and Rotating Crops 14

Fertility and Compost 16

Sowing and Propagating 18

Home-grown Salads 20

More Salads 22

Growing Peas and Beans 24

Growing Root Crops 26

The Cabbage Family 28

More Leaf Crops 30

Extending the Choice 32

Extending the
Choice Further 34

Greenhouses and Cold Frames 36

Greenhouse Crops 38

Saving Space with Mini-vegetables 40

Productive Containers 42

Growing Soft Fruit 44

Growing Tree Fruits 46

Pruning and Training Fruit 48

Planning a Herb Garden 50

Basic Culinary Herbs 52

Making a Herb Collection 54

Productive Ideas for Small Gardens 56

Dealing with Pests and Diseases 58

Weeds and Weeding 60

Index 62

Acknowledgments 64

INTRODUCTION

❖

THERE ARE MANY COMPELLING reasons for raising your own vegetables, fruit and herbs, not least the sensuous pleasure of contemplating them in all their orderly profusion, knowing they will ultimately end up on your plate.

Producing food from the garden has once more become an exciting enterprise that can arouse passionate interest and provide a great sense of achievement. Formerly banished to a separate enclosure, vegetables were for some time screened from sight at the bottom of the garden or even exiled to an allotment. Modern gardeners, however, are shedding preconceived notions and rediscovering an older tradition that recognized both the practical uses of flowering plants and the beauty of many edible crops, and mingling them together in artless harmony.

Tastes are changing, too. Foreign travel and a more cosmopolitan cuisine have introduced us to a wider range of food plants, more diverse and stimulating than the familiar range of staple crops. While the fruit and vegetables in our shops are inevitably limited to a relatively few easily managed varieties, there is an inspiring selection of unusual, exotic or old-fashioned crops now available to tempt every kitchen gardener.

Growing your own produce provides you with choice, giving you the chance to taste vegetables that are not only fresher but with more variety, colour and flavour than any you might buy. You can choose to grow large quantities of a few favourite, perhaps uncommon crops, for freezing or for sheer self-indulgence straight from the garden, or you might prefer to have a little of everything, well spaced out for continuity all season. How you tend your plants is

4

◁ **IT IS SURPRISING** *how much can be grown in a vegetable garden if you ensure that the ground is never left empty. With careful planning, you can be harvesting productive crops all through summer and into autumn.*

◁ **SUNNY CORNERS MAKE** *ideal kitchen garden sites, where plants can benefit from the warmth and shelter of boundary walls. And crops like cardoons, rhubarb, spinach and peas are as decorative as they are tasty.*

a further option: you might decide to grow 'organically', without depending on chemical treatments, to be sure that what you eat has had no unwanted additives.

Don't be daunted by the prospect of managing a kitchen garden. Most crops can be grown successfully with the same basic skills used elsewhere in the garden. Nor is a huge area of ground essential. If you do have plenty of space, you might prefer to gather all your various fruits together in a fruit cage for convenience, dedicate a separate plot exclusively to long rows of vegetables, or organise herbal plants in a formal decorative herb garden. But a small garden can still yield an abundance of produce – you can tuck a few strawberries or mixed summer lettuces in a fertile corner, line a path with parsley or carrots beneath a neat espalier apple, or train twining vegetables such as runner beans and outdoor cucumbers up vertical supports, where they will match the exuberance of any flowering climber.

Above all, you can guarantee freshness and flavour if you grow your own. Good cooking depends on the quality of the ingredients, many of which need harvesting in peak condition moments before they are wanted in the kitchen, to preserve their full, often short-lived perfection. The results could rekindle a jaded interest in real food, and make a satisfying climax to the pleasures of sowing, planting and tending your own kitchen garden produce.

Andi Clevely

ANDI CLEVELY

5

Designing a kitchen garden

Few gardeners have any choice about where to create a kitchen garden and, as most sites are less than perfect, it is important to know how to assess and improve the selected plot. Bear in mind that integrating food crops with other plants around the garden can sometimes be easier than keeping them separate and hidden from view.

6

△ **WHERE THERE** *is enough room in the garden, vegetables are traditionally grown in parallel rows, accessible both for cultivation and for harvest.*

PROVIDING SHELTER

Exposure to wind can have an adverse effect on crops, even light breezes reducing yields while strong winds stunt or damage plants. Many gardens are enclosed by fences, hedges or walls and these usually provide adequate shelter. Where crops are likely to be exposed, it is a good idea to protect them with a windbreak such as a hedge, perhaps of gooseberries or some other fruit, or an open fence on which climbing crops can be trained. Temporary or seasonal screens of sweet peas, Jerusalem artichokes, sweetcorn or raspberries are also effective.

ASPECT

Most crops like maximum sunlight for fast, healthy growth although some sensitive vegetables appreciate light shade in midsummer. Make sure any screen does not cast too much shade. The branches of overhanging trees can often be thinned to admit more sunlight, while excessively tall hedges may need to be reduced in height, for these cast shade and also confine still air on cold nights, turning a low-lying garden into a frost pocket. When designing your kitchen garden, note those areas where frost remains longest or which walls receive the most sunlight, and allocate crops where they are best suited.

△ **WEATHER CONDITIONS** *can be fickle, especially in late spring, and tender vegetables like marrows benefit from cloche protection after planting out.*

MAXIMIZING THE SPACE

❖

Fences and walls, including those of the house itself, offer extra space for growing crops: bush and tree fruits may be trained on walls, as can tall or climbing vegetables such as beans, peas, tomatoes and cucumbers. Most crops will thrive in pots and other containers, making it possible to assemble a collection of vegetables, herbs and fruit in a courtyard or even on a balcony.

△ **TRY GROWING CROPS** *informally in beds, combining and dispersing them with flowers.*

COPING WITH SLOPES

❖

Gardens are not always conveniently level, but this need not be a disadvantage when growing food crops: sloping sites are often less prone to frost, for example, and may also expose crops to more beneficial sunlight. Steep slopes can be difficult to cultivate, however, unless you divide them into a series of level terraces; alternatively, plant rows across the slope to prevent soil erosion by heavy rain.

THE LAYOUT

Crops may be grown in rows right across the cultivated area, but many gardeners prefer to divide the kitchen garden into small beds, arranged as squares edged with boards or bricks, or as long, narrow beds about 1.2m (4ft) wide so that the centre may be reached from each side without treading on the soil. Every system has its benefits and advocates, and part of the adventure of growing

your own is experimenting with various options. Allow for paths of a practical width that lead to all areas of the garden. You will need access to water, whether from a mains tap or rainwater stored in a tank or water butt, and you will probably find a utility corner necessary, preferably nearby, for a compost heap and toolshed.

PERENNIAL CROPS

When designing a kitchen garden, plan the positions of permanent crops first. Fruit trees and bushes are often used to define the layout, but other crops remain in the same place year after year, such as asparagus, globe artichokes, rhubarb and perennial herbs. Most annual vegetables move to fresh soil each season to avoid pest and disease problems.

▷ **THE IDEAL WIDTH** *of access paths depends on their use: 30cm (12in) is enough between herb beds but 90cm (3ft) may be needed for the comfortable passage of a laden wheelbarrow.*

The ornamental kitchen garden

There is great satisfaction to be found in straight, disciplined rows of crops, but vegetables, fruit and herbs can also be used as imaginative design elements of the mixed border or flower garden. Among them you will discover glorious colours and shapes to rival those of many purely ornamental plants.

△ COLOURFUL,
frilled lettuces grow with nasturtiums, onions and borage in timber-edged beds.

8 ▷ EXPLOIT THE
ornamental qualities of food plants by growing them in a geometric pattern of formal beds, defined by low box hedges.

THE BENEFITS

Medieval gardeners regarded crops as decorative in addition to being utility plants, and it was only the advent of the horse-hoe that established straight lines and wide spacings. If you abandon the hoe-a-row philosophy, you will find yields actually increase when plants are grown close together in small beds, their foliage touching and suppressing weeds as well as shading the soil. Pests and diseases often fail to find crops when they are integrated with other flowering plants, and it is easy to tuck just a few plants here and there, making up a cosmopolitan community that offers a little of everything.

DESIGN IDEAS

Several traditional garden styles can be adapted for the ornamental kitchen garden. **The potager** is a formally planned layout in which geometric beds are edged with dwarf vegetables or salad crops, then filled with flowers and crops arranged like summer bedding around a tall centrepiece. **The cottage garden** is an easy, informal patchwork of fruit, flowers and vegetables, combined in an apparently artless style that makes maximum use of every corner. Or you can borrow from **the grand kitchen garden** style in which straight paths divide the area into equal-sized beds, usually four to accommodate traditional rotation schemes, edged with flowers for cutting and enclosed with trained fruit trees.

In an existing garden you could start by introducing a fruiting variety wherever you want a small tree or shrub, or erect a cane wigwam of purple-

 ◁ LETTUCES GROW
companionably with flowering annuals such as marigolds. Wedge-shaped beds, edged with rope tiles, are separated by a framework of gravel paths.

podded peas or scarlet-flowered runner beans over untidy areas where bulb foliage is dying down. Sage and rosemary make exciting path-side shrubs, while annual crops can be combined with summer bedding – dwarf beans with geraniums, for example, or wallflowers with dwarf curly kale. A cordon-trained pear or thornless cut-leaf blackberry will clothe a pillar as prettily as a climbing rose, while paths may be edged with alpine strawberries, dwarf broad beans, mat-forming herbs like thyme and marjoram, or a mixture of carrots, parsley and dwarf bulbs.

THE VERTICAL DIMENSION

Many crops can be trained upwards. Fences and walls are often neglected, and yet their intensive use will sometimes double the potential of a small plot. Most fruits can be trained on fences and walls, including the walls of the house itself, and tall peas, beans, cucumbers, trailing squashes and outdoor tomatoes all benefit from the support and reflected warmth there. Thornless blackberries and loganberries, together with grape vines, can be trained on tripods, pillars and pergolas, or will scramble happily over an arbour shading a garden seat. These all occupy minimal space and cast so little shade that other vegetables and herbs may be grown at their base.

CONTAINER GARDENS

Although often seen as a substitute for open ground cultivation, containers extend both the cropping area and the decorative potential of any garden. Pots and tubs of herbs or salads can be clustered together on hard-surfaced areas, beside steps and doors for easy access or as ornamental groups on a patio; they are particularly useful for half-hardy crops that can be moved under cover when frost threatens. Half-barrels and other large containers may be planted with fruit trees or climbing crops, underplanted with a mixture of dwarf herbs and trailing bedding plants.

9

VEGETABLES IN THE BORDER

❖

Vegetable crops merge happily into flower borders if you place them according to their height.

FRONT OF BORDER: dwarf plants can be grown in rows or groups in front of all the others. Lettuces, beetroot and radicchio add colour and decorative leaf form that contrasts with ferny carrots and parsley.

MID-BORDER: asparagus, salsify and scorzonera are ideal here as flowering or foliage plants. Use rhubarb, Swiss chard and orache (mountain spinach) for eye-catching colour, combined with red Brussels sprouts and curly kale.

BACK OF BORDER: reserve space for tall crops such as globe artichokes, sweetcorn and herbs such as lovage, fennel and angelica, combined with tall peas and climbing beans on cane wigwams.

MAKING SPACE FOR FRUIT

❖

Trained fruits are the perfect choice where decorative highlights are needed, perhaps in the centre of a border or at the intersection of paths. Standard gooseberries and redcurrants make handsome individual features, while apples and pears (*right*) trained as cordons, espaliers and fans can flank paths or frame a gateway, especially if allowed to arch gracefully over the path. Try using rows of cordon-trained soft fruit as fruiting fences within the garden, or 'step-over' apples (single espaliers), 38–45cm (15–18in) high, as an edging to beds.

Developing a productive garden

*You do not need green fingers to be sure of raising tasty crops.
If you start with good-quality seeds and give healthy young plants
the right spacings and the routine care they need, the plants will
do the rest, especially if you concentrate on feeding the soil to
improve its fertility.*

THE IMPORTANCE OF LIME

Lime in the soil releases nutrients for plants to use and supports beneficial soil bacteria. The cabbage family in particular need plenty of lime, so when planting any brassica, first dress the soil with about 125g per sq m (4oz per sq yd) of garden lime. Lime also helps to break down clay soil if used regularly, although faster results are obtained by mixing together 80% gypsum (calcium sulphate) and 20% dolomite (magnesium limestone); apply at the same rate every autumn and spring until conditions improve.

10

◁ ORGANIC MATTER *can be added to the soil as garden compost. Make sure it is well rotted down before using.*

IMPROVING THE SOIL

Plants are only as good as the soil they grow in. Their roots prefer a moist, friable and fertile environment, and the more you can do to provide these conditions, the better your crops will be. Light, sandy soils are naturally friable but they need the addition of plenty of humus in the form of garden compost or well-rotted manure to keep them moist. The same materials will open up the texture of sticky, clay soils, allowing plant roots to penetrate deeply and use the nutrients. Fork in organic

△ USEFUL AIDS *to productivity include a fruit cage to keep birds off and a greenhouse for early sowings.*

materials in autumn, or simply spread them on the surface of bare ground or between rows as a protective mulch. The addition of lime can also improve some soils (*see box, above right*).

PLANTING

Transplant outdoors while plants are still young, about six weeks after sowing (see page 16) and when fully hardened

off by being gradually acclimatized to outdoor temperatures over 10–14 days. Make sure both plant and soil are moist. Then, using a trowel, dig out a hole large enough to take the rootball comfortably. Replace the soil over the rootball, firm into place and water the surrounding levelled soil; in dry weather, water the plant in the open hole and allow it to drain before refilling with soil. If the plants are large enough, mulch straight after planting to conserve moisture. Catch-cropping and inter-cropping (see page 21) helps maintain a continuous supply of salads and vegetables.

GENERAL CARE

Weeding Cultivated plants suffer in competition with weeds, which are more vigorous. Keep young crops weed-free until their foliage suppresses rivals by hoeing, mulching and weeding.

Watering Soaking plants thoroughly is more use than an occasional sprinkle. Leafy crops need regular watering, but other kinds benefit more from watering at critical times such as flowering or fruiting.

Feeding If the soil has been well-prepared with compost or manure, supplementary feeding will be needed only by the greediest crops. Choose a general (balanced) fertilizer for routine use, a nitrogen-rich feed for stimulating leaf growth after winter and a high-potash feed to improve flower and fruit quality.

KEEPING PLANTS HEALTHY

Pests and diseases are a natural part of garden life and cannot be kept at bay all the time. Problems are rarely serious if you take precautionary measures, such as using good-quality seeds and plants, choosing naturally resistant varieties, keeping the soil in good heart and clearing and destroying infected material promptly. Avoid the excessive use of chemicals that kill natural allies as well as pests. Use an environmentally friendly insecticide and fungicide.

PROTECTING CROPS

Cloches, cold frames or a greenhouse will extend the normal growing season by up to a month at each end, and will improve the quality of winter-hardy crops. Use cloches to warm the soil initially, to hasten germination and to protect growing plants from frost; in autumn they help ripen late crops or keep them growing for longer. A cold frame can be used for the same purpose, and also for hardening off crops before planting them out (see page 37).

MAXIMIZING YIELDS

Thorough initial soil preparation is the main secret of success, but there are other, additional ways to encourage high yields from your plot.
• Grow as wide a variety of plants as you can, because diversity reduces the risk of pests and diseases, and if one crop fails, others are likely to succeed.
• Cherish your plants. Check regularly – daily in summer – to make sure they have enough water and food to develop without faltering. Watch out for limp or lacklustre foliage, a sure sign of ailing.
• Harvest produce while it is young and immature: plants slow down as their crops finish ripening and do not always revive, whereas prompt and regular picking stimulates further growth.
• Never leave the ground empty. Plant a follow-on crop, sow a catch-crop of green manure for digging in when space is needed, or mulch the surface with compost to maintain good soil quality.

CHOOSING VARIETIES

Some vegetable varieties are trusted and well-established, others are new and often enticing. Both kinds have their merit in the kitchen garden, where experiment is part of the adventure of growing your own.

Try to choose varieties which suit your site and match your requirements. Seed catalogues usually state if a variety is particularly good for cold areas, light soils or exposed areas, for example. Some kinds are good for mass harvest

△ **A COLD FRAME** *is invaluable to overwinter, force or harden off plants ready for planting out. In summer it will provide extra growing room.*

and freezing or for close spacing in small areas, while many have some pest or disease resistance and are therefore favoured by organic gardeners. Hybrids, usually labelled as F1 or F2, are uniform, vigorous plants with predictable performance, but older, non-hybrid varieties can have superior flavour and may crop for longer.

If you have room, grow at least two varieties of any vegetable: choose one that is tried and tested (perhaps the best from last year), together with a new type for comparison. In that way you will gradually build up a collection of personal favourites. And remember that the heaviest overall yields often come from small, quick-maturing ('early') varieties, sown little and often throughout the season, and grown fast in moist, fertile conditions.

Always buy fresh seeds in good time for the first sowings each year, and test a sample of old stored seeds for viability – peas and beans will keep in a dry cool place for two years, cucumbers and marrows up to seven years, but parsnips, salsify and scorzonera do not keep well from one season to the next.

11

Digging and cultivation

Breaking up the ground where you intend to grow crops allows air, moisture, warmth and nutrients to penetrate deep into the soil and circulate around the roots, keeping them vigorous and in good health. Digging, forking and the other cultivation techniques described here are all ways of helping to create favourable conditions for efficient root growth.

IS DIGGING NECESSARY?

Deep digging every year is neither essential nor necessarily beneficial as it can destroy soil structure. The classic kitchen garden was divided into four quarters by cruciform paths: one quarter would be double dug each year in rotation, while the others were single dug or simply forked over, in a four-year sequence which maintained high fertility and good soil condition. Many gardeners find, however, that an initial deep preparation can be followed by annually forking or lightly digging just the top 'spit' (spade-depth) for ten years or more afterwards, until declining yields or impeded drainage indicate that deep digging is again advisable.

DOUBLE DIGGING

This involves trenching the ground two spits deep, to break up the subsoil and so allow deeper root penetration. Start by taking out a trench across one end of the plot, one spit deep, and barrow the excavated soil to the other end. With a fork, break up the subsoil in the bottom of the trench, and then spread a layer of compost or decayed manure over the loosened soil. Cover this with the topsoil from the next row, so producing a new trench in which you repeat the loosening, manuring and covering process. At the end, refill the final trench with the soil dug from the beginning of the plot. Any surface weeds and turf can be skimmed off and

◁ **PERSISTENT PUDDLES** *are a symptom of hard, waterlogged ground that needs digging or forking to speed drainage.*

buried under the top spit as you go, but perennial weeds and their root fragments should be removed; also take out any large stones. Dividing large plots lengthways makes the job less daunting psychologically and saves work, because the excavated soil at the start only needs moving sideways to be in position for the last trench.

SINGLE DIGGING

This is less arduous and loosens the soil to one spade-depth, enough to provide a workable tilth for routine sowing and planting; it is also the method used to mix in annual weed growth and dressings of manure or compost. You can dig across the plot in successive rows, inverting each spadeful of soil in its original position – this is the easiest approach in confined spaces or between existing rows of plants when you are preparing a strip for a new crop. Alternatively, excavate a trench as you would for double digging but leave the subsoil undisturbed. Dig the next strip and invert this topsoil into the empty trench in front of you. Manure or compost can be lightly mixed in at the

ESSENTIAL TOOLS

SPADE: A spade is essential for digging, and also serves to cut edges round plots, take out broad drills for legumes, earth up potatoes and move large amounts of soil. There are large-bladed digging spades and smaller border spades for light work, all fitted with a T- or D-shaped handle. Before buying, test a model for comfortable weight and balance. If you do a lot of digging – especially on clay – choose a blade made of stainless steel, as this is easy to keep clean.

FORK: As versatile as a spade for soil preparation and cultivation: there are digging and border forks, both available in stainless steel. A new fork with full-length tines is best for deep preparation, but keep an old one with sharp, worn tines for pricking over and other light surface work.

HOE: A Dutch hoe is most efficient for tilling the soil and is pushed just below the surface while you walk backwards. A draw hoe has a blade at right-angles to the handle, and is used to chop out weeds, take out seed drills and earth up plants.

△ **RAISED BEDS** *can solve the problem of shallow, inhospitable soil and eliminate the need for digging.*

DIGGING TIPS

❖

• Only dig for as long as you are comfortable, rest often during the work, and stop before you are tired.

• Cleaning your spade at the ends of rows reduces effort, and makes a good opportunity to pause and straighten your back.

• Dig heavy ground in autumn and leave it rough for the frost to break down large clods; light soils are more fragile and best dug in spring or just before sowing or planting.

• When digging stony ground, leave the last trench open and rake the surface stones into this.

same time, or you can leave that stage until later, when forking the surface to a tilth just before sowing or planting.

FORKING

On very good, friable soil, a garden fork is an acceptable substitute for a spade,

◁ **FORKING IS A CRUCIAL STAGE** *in the process of cultivating and improving the texture of soil that is lumpy or compacted.*

provided you always insert the tines to their full depth, loosening and stirring the topsoil as you go and mixing in some kind of organic matter at regular intervals. For all soils, forking is used to break down large clods to a crumbly texture suitable for raking; to mix in mulches and top-dressings of compost or manure; and to uproot small weeds and maintain soil condition during the season by loosening the trodden surface. This light forking, often called 'pricking over', leaves the surface in a well-broken state ready for planting or preparing a seedbed. It also allows rain to penetrate more easily deep into the ground, and should be done wherever puddles tend to linger, especially in well-trodden pathways between rows.

HOEING

Although most gardeners think of a hoe as a light flat-bladed tool used to lightly scuffle the soil and keep it weed-free, the term covers a range of tools, quite varied in appearance but all designed for routine surface cultivation. Regular hoeing disturbs small weed seedlings, chops the tops off larger weeds, and maintains a fine aerated tilth that admits rain and irrigation, while delaying drying out to some extent. This is a valuable aid to sustained crop growth and avoids the prospect of prolonged hand-weeding at a later stage. Soil that has been dug over, forked, then left to settle for a week or two needs only light superficial tilling with a hoe before it is ready for planting or sowing. Hoe when the weather is dry and sunny to control weeds; just before rain if there is a surface crust that might obstruct water penetration; and just after a summer shower to prevent rapid evaporation.

13

Planning and rotating crops

If you decide to grow just a few lettuces or perhaps a row of parsley, the plants can be tucked in almost anywhere in the garden. But if you have more ambitious plans, they will benefit from a little forethought to ensure you make the best use of limited space, avoid a gap or a glut in supply, and escape problems that may arise if you grow the same crop continuously in one place.

PLANNING FOR CONTINUITY

Many vegetables are started at about the same time. Mid-spring is a favourite season for sowing a wide range of crops, and there is a real risk of filling the available space early in the year and leaving no room for later crops, so temper your enthusiasm with a little long-term planning. Estimate how long each variety will occupy the ground and when it will be ready (seed packets tell you this basic information), and spread out your sowings to provide a steady supply of produce.

Precision is difficult in the kitchen garden, so be flexible and allow for poor weather (this, rather than the calendar,

will often govern sowing times). Save some seeds for resowing in case of failed germination, use cloches to extend the growing season early and late (*see page 6*), and be prepared to start plants in pots or trays while they wait for space. If there is not enough room for several successive sowings of a crop such as peas or Brussels sprouts, try growing a single large batch of a good freezing variety instead – this can be cleared in a single harvest while in peak condition for a continuous supply from the freezer.

SPRINTERS AND LONG-DISTANCE CROPS

Vegetables grow at different rates, some taking much longer than others. In general, early or small varieties sprint to maturity compared with maincrop and over-wintered varieties, which often need months rather than weeks to finish their growth. In a small garden, you could concentrate on repeated sowings of 'sprinters' for

FAST CROPS	
cutting lettuces	4-5 weeks
radishes	5 weeks
turnips (small)	8 weeks
heading lettuces	8 weeks
bunching carrots	10 weeks
early peas	10 weeks
kohl rabi	10 weeks
courgettes	10-12 weeks
early potatoes	10-12 weeks
French beans	10-12 weeks
beetroot	12 weeks
calabrese	12 weeks
runner beans	12 weeks

SLOW CROPS	
broad beans	20 weeks
cauliflowers	20 weeks
maincrop potatoes	22 weeks
onions	24 weeks
celery	28 weeks
kale	28 weeks
leeks	28 weeks
Brussels sprouts	30 weeks
spring cabbage	32 weeks
sprouting broccoli	40 weeks

maximum yields, or grow a few favourite long-term vegetables with plenty of space left in between for an opportunist sowing of a fast variety. The growing times listed above are typical averages for a cool climate.

SPACING

Every crop needs enough space to develop fully and healthily, but the distances between plants and rows recommended on seed packets and in

◁ **SMALL FORMAL BEDS** *simplify planning and keep apart unrelated plants with different growth rates.*

14

△ **CROP ROTATION**, *wih all its benefits, is easy to manage if you divide your plot into separate, clearly defined compartments.*

books are often generous, to allow easy access for cultivation. Be prepared to experiment, because slightly closer spacing can frequently increase total yields from your plot; at even greater densities, size begins to decline, which may be an advantage if you prefer a lot of small plants for gathering while young. But when thinning seedlings, do not be tempted to leave root crops such as carrots and turnips closer than recommended within the row, as they may produce a lot of leaves and no usable roots. Cabbages, lettuces and other leafy vegetables can be planted at twice the usual density if you cut alternate plants while still immature, leaving the rest to heart up as normal.

SITING PERENNIALS

Perennial vegetables need careful siting if they are not to get in the way of future plans – asparagus plants, for example, can remain productive for 30 years or more. You could dedicate one end of a bed to these permanent crops, or confine them to a row at the back of a bed or beside a path. Many make attractive feature plants, however, and asparagus, seakale, globe artichokes and cardoons are dramatic foliage plants that

blend effectively in flower beds. With its bold leaves and coloured stems, rhubarb can be an exciting component of pond-side plantings, or you might include it with several other perennial crops in a larger herb garden. The tall, robust stems of Jerusalem artichokes and perennial broccoli also make useful windbreaks to shelter the more vulnerable vegetables and early sowings from cold winds.

CROP ROTATION

Pests, diseases and deficiency disorders may eventually appear if you grow a particular crop, or its close relative, in the same place year after year. Crop rotation is a precaution designed to avoid these risks by moving susceptible plants to new sites each year, so preventing most serious health problems from taking hold. Whole groups of related plants were traditionally moved around in a set sequence and on a regular basis (the classic arrangement is a 3- or 4-year cycle), with the soil prepared annually

---

ROTATION CROPS

PEAS AND BEANS: This group, often called legumes, likes deeply dug, fertile ground with a little lime added, but there is no need to add a lot of compost or manure before planting because their roots manufacture nitrogen from the air. Celery, tomatoes and spinach may also be grown with this group.

CABBAGE FAMILY: The brassicas include cauliflowers, broccoli, kale and Brussels sprouts. They need firm soil, plenty of lime and high fertility, so dig in manure or compost in winter, then lime the soil at planting time. Alternatively, grow brassicas after legumes – just cut down the peas and beans, topdress with fertilizer, and plant into the undisturbed soil.

ROOT CROPS: Carrots, beetroot, parsnips and radishes belong to this group. They dislike recently manured ground but need a well-broken soil for their roots to penetrate easily. They are useful for mopping up fertilizer residues from previous groups, and need little preparation apart from loosening the soil with a fork.

Potatoes belong with root crops, but are often grown as a separate rotation group in deeply dug and well-manured ground.

15

to meet the specific preferences of the vegetable group to be grown. Although sound in principle and very effective in a large kitchen garden, this practice is too rigid for small plots or numbers of plants, and you can usually achieve the same results if you simply avoid growing an individual crop or one from its group of relatives in the same place in two consecutive seasons.

Fertility and compost

Healthy, vigorous growth depends on the presence in the soil of a balanced supply of varied plant foods, in a form that is readily available to the hungry roots. You can provide this lifeline and ensure quality crops by adding manures, fertilizers and compost, often by processing waste materials from the home and garden.

HUMUS

Soil is made up of a number of mineral ingredients, together with an organic material called humus. This is partly decayed animal or vegetable matter, which supplies nutrients as it decomposes, absorbs water and so prevents rapid drying in hot or windy weather. Humus provides the dark colour of rich, fertile soils – compare the pale, relatively infertile subsoil at the bottom of a planting hole with the darker, more fibrous texture of the humus-rich upper layer.

You can feed plants directly with chemical fertilizers and they will grow reasonably well, but they will lack resilience in extreme weather and will not have the overall positive health displayed by plants grown in soil high in organic matter. This is because humus also sustains a lavish population of ground fauna such as worms and beneficial bacteria which, between them, create good soil structure and texture, which in turn stimulate active plant growth. Feed the soil with plenty of organic matter, supplement this with an occasional feed, and your crops will thrive with little further encouragement.

MANURES

The classic source of bulky organic matter is farmyard manure, a highly efficient soil conditioner that adds body to light sandy soils and opens up sticky clay, as well as supplying a small amount of nutrients. If fresh, it should be stacked until well-rotted before it is dug in during the autumn to blend into the soil over winter, ready for the next season. For gardeners living in towns or with very small plots, fresh manure is an impractical option. But an excellent substitute is composted manure, supplied in bags for adding to the soil at any time. Regular top-dressings, lightly stirred in whenever you are about to

△ **DIGGING IN** *partly rotted manure improves the structure of all soils and supplies nourishment.*

sow or plant, will gradually add some humus and instantly available nutrients to the soil. Spent mushroom compost is another alternative manure, already well-rotted and ideal as a mulch or soil conditioner – it is particularly suitable for clay soils as it has a high lime content, but avoid excessive use around acid-loving plants such as raspberries.

FERTILIZERS

Use fertilizers to supplement the organic input to the soil, rather than as the sole source of fertility. They are concentrated and rapidly absorbed for very quick

16

△ **ALL PLANTS DECOMPOSE** *into beneficial humus and minerals, but green manure species make a very rich contribution to soil quality.*

results, but are soon washed from the soil by rain. There are chemical and 'organic' feeds, some delivered in a slow-release form which supplies a gentle trickle of nutrients all season. Granular and powdered fertilizers are sprinkled around growing plants or broadcast for raking in before sowing and planting. Liquid feeds are quick-acting tonics that you water or spray on the plants when they are in immediate need – during or after a drought, for example, or when limp and yellowing foliage indicates starvation. Fertilizers that contain trace elements supply the most complete diet of nutrients.

GREEN MANURES

Green manure plants produce a large amount of leafy material that is dug in to decay as a soil conditioner and mild fertilizer. They are particularly useful as a catch-crop wherever ground is left empty for six weeks or more between crops, or as a live mulch to protect bare soil over winter when heavy rain might otherwise leach nutrients and harm the soil structure. Keep a supply of mustard, phacelia or crimson clover to sow as a catch-crop during the growing season, and field beans, winter tares or winter rye for sowing in autumn and turning in the following spring. Before digging them in, cut or tread down the plants and sprinkle them with a dressing of dried blood or sulphate of ammonia to accelerate decomposition.

ORGANIC MULCHING

A mulch of organic material such as well-rotted manure, garden compost, mushroom compost or composted bark is a protective physical barrier against extreme weather, rapid evaporation and weed growth. It is also a valuable source of fertility: as it decomposes it is drawn into the soil slowly by worms or mixed in when planting. Non-digging enthusiasts depend on a heavy mulch to preserve soil texture and supply nutrients, but all gardeners could profit from its beneficial action. Spread a 5cm (2in) layer over cultivated soil, between plants or where the ground is left empty, and top up

Organic mulch

to this depth in spring and autumn. Some of the mulch can be stirred in when transplanting vegetables, or you can simply draw the material to one side and replace it after planting.

17

MAKING COMPOST
❖

Home-made garden compost recycles plant and household waste into an inexpensive and effective soil conditioner and source of fertility. Use a large container, which may be a sturdy timber box, a proprietary plastic bin or a simple wire netting enclosure lined with cardboard, and stand this on the soil to allow access to worms. Collect enough waste to complete a layer about 20cm (8in) deep, ideally mixing soft materials such as grass clippings and annual weeds with more fibrous stems or straw to avoid compaction. Cover this with a thin layer of nitrogen-rich activator, such as nettles in summer or pelleted poultry manure in winter, and continue in the same way until the container is full. Make sure the contents are moist, and top with an insulating cover of old carpet, blanket or perforated plastic to retain heat. Turn the heap after three months to mix the sides in with the more decomposed heart, to produce a more consistent compost. Do not include large amounts of tree leaves: these are best rotted on their own to make leafmould, a superb soil conditioner and ingredient of potting compost.

Sowing and propagating

Although propagation is a skill that might intimidate some gardeners, it is part of every plant's life cycle. Whenever you sow vegetable seeds or divide a clump of herbs, you are assisting in a completely natural process of plant reproduction, but under carefully controlled, ideal conditions that should give a crop the best possible start to its hard-working life.

GROWING OPTIONS

Vegetables are mostly raised from seeds, sown either where the plants are to grow, or in containers under glass. Sowing indoors allows you greater control over growth if conditions outside are unsuitable – where the ground is cold and wet, for example, or while frost is a serious threat early and late in the season. The two basic sowing techniques are shown below.

Some herbs are also started from seed, though others begin life as cuttings or divisions taken from older plants. Soft fruits are grown from seed or, more usually, cuttings, and top fruit by grafting a choice variety on a particular rootstock (*see page 42*). Most of these methods are easy and dependable if you follow the basic procedures. You can avoid this growth stage altogether if you do not have the inclination or the necessary facilities, and an increasingly popular option is to buy young plants or small plug seedlings, plant these where they are to grow, then discard them after harvest. But most gardeners find that propagating plants is satisfying and irresistible, and indeed essential if you want to grow choice or elusive varieties.

SOWING VEGETABLE SEEDS INDOORS

You can make an early start and retain greater control over later batches of plants by sowing in fresh seed or multi-purpose compost in pots under cover.

1 *Fill the pot or tray with compost and level the top, then tap or lightly firm to settle the contents; water and allow to drain. Sow sparingly on the surface and cover with a thin layer of compost (use vermiculite if light needed to germinate). Cover with glass or plastic; keep warm.*

2 *When the seedlings are large enough to handle, hold each one carefully by a leaf and transplant, singly, to small pots or 5cm (2in) apart in trays of compost; water in and keep shaded for a few days. Or sow direct in small pots or cell trays, large seeds singly and others in small pinches.*

SOFTWOOD CUTTINGS

These cuttings are prepared from the tips of new shoots, any time between early spring and late summer while growth is active. This is the quickest way to multiply most shrubby perennial herbs, and the only reliable method for named varieties, especially variegated kinds that do not come true to type from seed. Use a very sharp knife to cut off the end 10cm (4in) of the shoot, trim the lower leaves from this and cut the base cleanly just under a leaf joint. Dip the bottom end in rooting hormone and shake off any surplus, then insert the cutting to half its length in a potful of gritty cuttings compost – you can usually space out several in an 11.5cm (4½in) pot. Water in and keep in a lightly shaded position until new pale growth indicates successful rooting. Evergreen herbs are best propagated by

SOWING OUTDOORS

❖

Before sowing direct into the ground, prepare a seedbed by forking out any weeds, dressing the surface with 60g per sq m (2oz per sq yd) general fertilizer, then raking to produce a fine level tilth that is free of stones.

1 *Using a taut line or the edge of a board as a guide, inscribe a straight channel (drill) at the correct depth for the seeds. Water the drill first in dry weather.*

2 *Either sprinkle the seeds sparingly along the full length of the drill or space a small group of seeds at a measured distance apart.*

3 *Carefully cover the seeds with fine soil, gently tamping and watering this into place, and label the row. Protect with netting if birds are a problem.*

semi-ripe cuttings, taken around midsummer and made in the same way from sideshoots twisted off with a portion of the old stem (a 'heel'), which is left on to aid rooting.

HARDWOOD CUTTINGS

In late autumn or early winter, soft fruit bushes such as blackcurrants and gooseberries can be multiplied from woody shoots cut from the current year's growth (look for the paler stems). Trim them to about 20-30cm (8-12in) long, by removing the soft tip and cutting the base below a leaf joint. Push a spade into a vacant, sheltered corner

▷ FRESHLY SOWN SEEDS *and transplanted seedlings are vulnerable to weather extremes, especially if they were started inside. Introduce them gently to outdoor temperatures by progressively hardening them off in a cold frame.*

of the plot and work it back and forth to make a V-shaped slit trench. Trickle a little sharp sand or grit in the bottom for good drainage, space the cuttings about 30cm (12in) apart, upright and

with just the upper third above ground, and firm them in with your heel. Cuttings of blackcurrants are always buried with their buds intact to encourage new stems from below ground, but the lower buds are best removed from other fruits to produce a single, clean stem for easy maintenance. The cuttings should be well-rooted by the following autumn.

DIVISION

As its name suggests, this method involves dividing a rootstock into smaller portions. Clump-forming herbs such as marjoram and lemon balm are simply cut or pulled apart into portions, either where they grow or after lifting, and the young outer pieces replanted elsewhere. Rhubarb crowns are split with a spade into pieces, each with a fat live bud, while vegetables such as globe artichokes and cardoons produce young offsets that can be separated with a fork from the side of the old crown. Winter is the best time for division, although it can also succeed in spring or autumn.

19

Home-grown salads

Freshness and variety are essential for a well-made salad, and you can ensure both qualities by raising your own salad crops. A host of flavours, colours and leafy delights may be gathered from a small bed throughout the season and, with the help of cloches, fleece or a cold frame, this profusion can be extended year-round.

LETTUCE

Different varieties come in attractive guises. Butterheads (Bib lettuces) are soft-textured and grow faster than upright cos (romaine) varieties; crispheads (icebergs) enjoy plenty of water and sunshine; while loose-leaf kinds may be cut repeatedly from an early age. Red, brown and frilled lettuces add tempting colour and form to the salad bowl.

Cultivation

Sow little and often, 1cm (½in) deep in rows 15cm (6in) apart and thin seedlings to 15–23cm (6–9in) apart according to variety. Keep weed-free, water as required and feed two or three times during growth. Start harvesting early as batches usually mature together, about 8–12 weeks after sowing, and may then deteriorate quickly. Either gather a few leaves at a time from loose-leaf kinds, or cut complete plants down to a 2.5cm (1in) stump to allow for regrowth.

RADISHES

Summer varieties with small red, white or bicoloured roots mature in just three to four weeks and need frequent sowing for continuity. Larger Japanese (mooli) types and winter radishes are sown after the longest day for use three months later. Special low-temperature varieties may be grown under glass in winter.

Cultivation

Sow thinly, 1cm (½in) deep in short rows 15cm (6in) apart, every two weeks outdoors and four to six weeks in autumn and winter under glass. Thin seedlings to

△ **RADISHES CAN BE GROWN** *as a catch-crop between rows of lettuce.*

2.5–7.5cm (1–3in) apart while still small. Water regularly for fast growth; crops on well-prepared soil need no feeding. Harvest summer kinds as soon as they are large enough, mooli varieties when 15cm (6in) long. Leave winter varieties in the ground and use as needed.

SALAD ONIONS

Often known as spring onions, these non-bulbing varieties can be available almost all year round and add a savoury flourish to salads. They like fertile conditions and may be grown as an edging to beds.

Cultivation

Sow every three to four weeks in spring and summer, 1cm (½in) deep, in rows 20cm (8in) apart or as 7.5-cm (3-in) wide bands 15cm (6in) apart; thin seedlings to 2.5cm (1in) apart. Sow in late summer for spring use, and cover

◁ **LETTUCE IS AN** *easily grown crop, with a range of enticing varieties. Frilly-leaved kinds are good value and stay usable over a long season.*

crops with cloches over winter. Weed regularly and water when dry. Harvest as soon as large enough, starting with the biggest thinnings, then pull up alternate plants, leaving the others to gain size.

OTHER SALAD CROPS

Many leaf crops can be used in varying amounts to enliven salads: these are just a few of the more popular kinds.

Chicory

Refreshingly bitter, crisp leaves in loose, round heads or tight, conical chicons. Red-leafed radicchio and green sugar-loaf chicory are grown in the same way as lettuce. Witloof chicory is sown in late spring, in rows 15cm (6in) apart, thinned to 20cm (8in) apart in the rows.

Red-leaf chicory 'Prima Rosa'

Dig up the roots in autumn, trim off the leaves, plant in pots and force in warmth and total darkness to produce blanched chicons.

Corn salad

Sometimes called lamb's lettuce (*Valerianella locusta*), this is a mild leaf crop sown in late summer for winter and spring use. Sow in drills 15cm (6in) apart and thin seedlings to 10cm (4in) apart; transplant thinnings to a cold frame or greenhouse for protection.

Land cress

An easily grown substitute for watercress, land or American cress is sown in spring for summer use, and in late summer for picking over winter. Grow 15cm (6in) apart each way and keep moist at all times. Plants self-seed and produce seedlings that may be transplanted.

Summer purslane

Portulaca oleracea has succulent, tangy leaves that may be cut or picked repeatedly over a long period. Sow by broadcasting seed in early summer in a warm, sunny position, thin seedlings to about 5cm (2in) apart and harvest as a cut-and-come-again crop.

CUT-AND-COME-AGAIN

❖

Most leafy salad vegetables can be grown as seedling crops, sown in strips or patches at close spacing. Harvest the plant tops with scissors when about 8cm (3in) tall, working across the patch gradually and leaving 2.5-cm (1-in) high stumps to regrow for a further two or three cuttings. Surplus lettuce, chicory and endive seeds can be blended to make your own salad mixture.

TIPS FOR SUCCESS

LETTUCE

○ Site summer lettuces in light shade, but choose an open, sunny position at other seasons.
○ Keep consistently moist, but do not overwater.
○ Seeds become dormant in hot weather; make summer sowings in the afternoon and cover with damp newspaper for 24 hours to keep cool.
○ Mulching plants on dry soils prevents them from bolting to seed early.

RADISHES

○ Radishes are brassicas, so do not grow where there is club-root disease.
○ Roots grow best in a bright position, but midsummer crops will appreciate light shade.
○ If plants run up to flower, leave them to produce their edible seedpods.
○ Watch out for slugs and flea beetles attacking seedlings.

SALAD ONIONS

○ Grow parsley nearby as a traditional deterrent against onion fly.
○ Sow very early crops under glass in modules, a few seeds to each cell.
○ Spring- and summer-sown crops take about eight weeks to mature, over-wintered plants 30–36 weeks.
○ Choose a hardy variety for late-summer sowings.

CATCH-CROPPING AND INTER-CROPPING

Maintain a continuous supply by sowing fast-maturing crops such as radishes, corn salad, land cress and turnips wherever ground is likely to be empty for a few weeks before or between other crops. Alternatively, allow similar crops to take advantage of the space between rows of slow-growing vegetables while their plants are still small. Use these empty spaces to sow seedlings for transplanting later, or to grow young plants on for a few weeks.

21

More salads

After trying some of the easier kinds, you will probably want to explore the wider choice of tasty salads. New varieties, especially from other cultures and cuisines, are continually being introduced as part of the process of transforming the basic salad into a gourmet experience. Kitchen gardeners are well placed to take advantage of this exciting trend.

ENDIVE

Recent curly (frisée) varieties of this chicory relative are fairly hardy and may be grown in place of traditional broad-leaf (Batavian or escarole) winter kinds, as well as for normal summer use. Plants develop heavy hearts that are self-blanching, which reduces their natural bitterness to a refreshing piquancy.

Cultivation

Sow outdoors between mid-spring and late summer in the same way as lettuce, but thin to 23–30cm (9–12in) apart. If hearts do not turn pale naturally, cover each one with an inverted dinner plate for 10–14 days before cutting. In mid-autumn protect late plants with fleece or cloches, or grow in a frame.

CELERY

Self-blanching and green (American) varieties supply unrivalled crunchiness and distinctive flavour to summer salads, and a later batch will extend the harvest right through autumn if protected from frost. Trench varieties are the only reliable source of winter celery, but these are labour-intensive and difficult to grow well.

Cultivation

Surface-sow under glass 10 weeks before the last frosts, and prick out in small pots or 5cm (2in) apart in

◁ **TRENCH CELERY**

may be grown on the surface provided the stems are blanched in a jacket made of paper or corrugated cardboard.

MIXED SALADS

An economical way to add variety to the salad bowl is to buy a packet of mixed ('saladini') seeds. An increasing range of blends – Italian, French, oriental, crisp or spicy, for example – is now available. Either grow as a cut-and-come-again crop (see page 21), or prick out a selection of seedlings and plant as for lettuces so that you can mix leaves from selected mature heads.

trays. Harden off and plant out 23cm (9in) apart in blocks to encourage blanching. Water lavishly in dry weather and feed at midsummer. Sow again in late spring for autumn use. Plants are ready from 8 weeks after planting.

SORREL

Ordinary sorrel is a very sharp, acidic herb, high in vitamin C and used like spinach, but French or buckler-leafed sorrel (*Rumex scutatus*) has a more refined flavour with a citrus tang. Grow it as an annual or perennial, and keep a few plants in containers to bring indoors for prolonged pickings.

Cultivation

Sow outdoors during spring, and thin annual crops to 20cm (8in) apart, perennials 38cm (15in) each way. Keep fairly moist in dry weather. Pick small quantities of younger leaves just before they are needed. Rejuvenate ageing perennial clumps by simply dividing the crowns in spring, using a sharp knife.

ROCKET

The leaves of cultivated salad rocket have a rich, spicy flavour, and are cut while still small for mixing with other salad leaves. Wild rocket, more pungent and increasing in popularity, is used in the same way. Plants may run to seed quickly in hot weather, so grow little and often, in light shade during the summer months.

Cultivation

Sow outdoors between early spring and late summer, and do not thin the seedlings. You can pick individual leaves or cut whole plants when they are 10cm (4in) high, but leave 2.5cm (1in) stumps for regrowth. The latest sowings will survive mild frosts if covered in mid-autumn.

OUTDOOR TOMATOES

There are hundreds of classic heritage varieties with varied shapes and colours, and nearly all are best grown outdoors as they become too leggy and space-consuming under glass. Some of the least good-looking kinds – with greenish, black or misshapen fruits – are in fact the most delicious.

Cultivation

Start about 8 weeks before the last frosts. Sow, prick out and plant as for greenhouse varieties (see page 38),

◁ ROCKET PLANTS *make attractive rosettes of shapely leaves. Cut the youngest for use, leaving the tough, older foliage to support further growth.*

spacing them 45–50cm (18–20in) apart in a sunny, sheltered position. Train them like greenhouse cordons, but stop growing tips after 3–4 trusses; tuck straw under bush varieties to keep fruit clean. Pick all ungathered fruits when the first frost threatens.

OUTDOOR CUCUMBERS

Traditional outdoor (ridge) cucumbers are short, fat and slightly prickly, but recent varieties, especially Japanese kinds, are as long and slim as greenhouse cucumbers, or round like yellow apples. Train them on trellis or wigwams of bamboo canes as decorative climbers, and harvest regularly to sustain cropping.

Cultivation

Either buy plants and harden them off for planting 60cm (24in) apart when the weather has warmed up, or start as for greenhouse varieties (page 38), 4–5 weeks before the last frosts. Grow in a warm, sheltered position, training the stems on canes or trellis, and pinch out the growing tips when they reach the top. Clear fruits before the first frosts, or earlier if mildew strikes.

▷ FRUITING CUCUMBERS *are heavy plants, so tie the main stems securely to strong, upright canes. Leave the sideshoots to support themselves by their tendrils.*

TIPS FOR SUCCESS

ENDIVE
❍ In hot, dry gardens choose a variety noted for its resistance to bolting.
❍ When thinning rows, save the surplus seedlings and transplant elsewhere.
❍ Make sure hearts are dry before blanching, or they may start to rot.

CELERY
❍ Transplant into a soil-based cold frame for an extra pale blanch and longer frost protection.
❍ Consistent watering prevents early bolting and guarantees crisp stalks.

ROCKET
❍ Cut back unused plants regularly to avoid flowering, older plants become very strongly flavoured.
❍ Sow in mid-autumn under glass or in pots on a window-sill for use all winter and early spring.
❍ The flowers can be used like the leaves; let a few set seed, to sow later.

SORREL
❍ Hot sunlight makes the leaves bitter; grow some in shade for summer use.
❍ Sow or divide plants in late summer; pot up for winter harvest indoors.
❍ Use stainless steel to cut sorrel, as iron turns the leaves black.

OUTDOOR TOMATOES
❍ After planting out, protect plants until the weather becomes reliable.
❍ In cold gardens, train plants against a sunny wall for extra warmth.
❍ Avoid irregular watering, which causes splitting and blossom end rot.

OUTDOOR CUCUMBERS
❍ Bury plenty of compost or rotted manure at each individual site.
❍ Mulch to conserve moisture.
❍ With outdoor varieties there is no need to remove male flowers or prevent pollination.

23

Growing peas and beans

High in protein and delicious when harvested fresh from the garden, peas and beans of all kinds are decorative vegetables that are typical of the kitchen garden in summer. They are good for the soil too, because bacteria in their roots draw nitrogen from the air and leave it in the ground for later crops to use.

△ **COLOURED**

VARIETIES *of bean, such as these golden waxpods, are as prolific as plain green kinds and look attractive when served.*

▽ **PEAS AND**

DWARF BEANS

24 *enjoy the same soil preparation and can be grown side by side, the peas supported on canes and string to aid rapid growth and easy picking.*

PEAS

Round-seeded varieties are hardy and used for autumn or late winter sowings, whereas the sweeter, wrinkled kinds are sown from spring onwards. Ordinary peas produce fat green or purple pods filled with seeds for shelling, but some have flat (mangetout) and cylindrical (sugar-snap) fibreless pods that are picked young and eaten whole.

Cultivation

Sow 4–5cm (1½–2in) deep and 7.5cm (3in) apart in strips 23cm (9in) wide, in deeply dug and well-manured ground; spread lime on the surface if the soil is acid. Firm the soil after sowing and net against birds. Support when the first tendrils appear, with canes and netting or twiggy sticks that match the variety's height. Weed regularly and mulch when about 15cm (6in) high. Water in dry weather, especially when plants carry flowers or pods; harvest pods before they become large and fibrous. After cropping, cut plants at ground level and leave the roots to decay.

BROAD BEANS

Easy, prolific and reliably hardy, these are the first summer vegetables in most gardens. Both the young green, white or red

seeds and also the immature pods are eaten. There are tall or short varieties, some robust enough to sow in autumn for the earliest crops.

Cultivation

Make two or three monthly sowings from late winter onwards, burying the large seeds 5cm (2in) deep and 23cm (9in) apart each way in well-dug, well-manured soil, limed if acid; also sow in mid- to late autumn for overwintering, or start seeds in pots under glass in midwinter. Mulch plants to prevent soils drying out, and support tall varieties with stakes and string. Water if necessary while plants are flowering and cropping. Start harvesting pods for cooking whole when about 7.5cm (3in) long, two to three weeks later for shelling.

RUNNER BEANS

With their vivid scarlet blooms, these are perhaps the most ornamental beans. They crop very heavily on fertile soils where their roots are always cool and moist. Provide strong support for the heavy top growth.

△ **RUNNER BEANS**

were first grown as colourful annual climbers rather than productive vegetables and are ideal to train over an archway.

◁ CLIMBING BEANS
sown into these degradable whalehide pots can be planted out without any root disturbance.

FRENCH BEANS

Both dwarf and tall, twining kinds are grown for a number of purposes: pods may be eaten whole or sliced, or can be shelled for their seeds, either fresh (flageolets) or for drying (haricot beans). Pods are flat or cylindrical in various colours, often dramatically speckled.

Cultivation

Either sow direct outdoors about a month before the last frosts or start seeds in small individual pots under glass. Dig and manure the ground thoroughly before sowing seeds or planting out young plants. Give support in the form of canes, arranged either in rows or in the form of a wigwam. Water the plants twice-weekly from the time the flowers first open.

Cultivation

Sow in pots under glass or outdoors in rich, deeply dug soil three to four weeks before the last frosts. Sow 4–5cm (1½–2in) deep, spacing climbers as for runner beans and dwarf kinds 23cm (9in) apart each way or every 10cm (4in) in rows 45cm (18in) apart. Grow on like runner beans. Start picking before the seeds are prominent in the pods and repeat every three to four days.

SUPPORTING CLIMBING BEANS

❖

Sturdy support is essential for the lush top growth. Use 2.5m (8ft) canes or treated 5 x 5cm (2 x 2in) timber set firmly in the ground and tied securely at the top for stability. Proprietary fittings are available for securing the tops of wigwams and also for joining the canes in short rows, sometimes with built-in watering arrangements.

Sow seeds 5cm (2in) deep and 15–20cm (6–8in) apart at the foot of each supporting cane.

Mulch with straw or well-rotted garden compost after germination or planting, to conserve moisture.

Start harvesting when beans are about 15cm (6in) long and check every two to three days for further pods.

TIPS FOR SUCCESS

PEAS
❍ Sow maincrop and mangetout varieties once or twice in spring, early kinds every 3 weeks for succession.
❍ For earliest pickings, start hardy varieties outdoors in late winter under cloches or in pots in a cold frame.
❍ Peas like cool conditions, so keep moist and give midsummer crops light shade.
❍ Space seeds carefully: peas dislike overcrowding.

BROAD BEANS
❍ Pinch off the tips of main stems when the first pods have formed to hasten maturity and deter blackfly.
❍ Sow dwarf varieties up to late summer in cool shade for a late crop.
❍ Save surplus seeds for sowing as a green manure crop in spare ground.
❍ In cold gardens cover autumn sowings with cloches or fleece.

RUNNER BEANS
❍ Runner beans cannot stand frost, so make sure pot-grown plants are hardened off before planting out.
❍ In clean, fertile ground, plants can grow in the same place each year with permanent supports.
❍ Dwarf varieties, or tall kinds kept pinched back to 45cm (18in) high, need no supports but benefit from a straw mulch to keep pods clean.
❍ Grow with a few sweet peas to improve the beans' chances of pollination.

FRENCH BEANS
❍ Harvest lasts for 6–8 weeks, so make two or three further sowings of dwarf kinds for continuity.
❍ Earth up stems and support dwarf varieties with twiggy sticks to keep crops clean.
❍ For haricot beans, leave the pods on the plant until brown, hang up complete plants to dry, then shell out the seeds for storing.

25

Growing root crops

The most popular root crops for garden cultivation are beetroot, carrots, parsnips and potatoes. They give good yields from a small area and share a preference for light, open, well-cultivated soil, which their roots can penetrate with little effort, together with a reasonable degree of fertility.

△ **FRESHLY HARVESTED PARSNIPS** *have a sweet flavour. They can be left in the ground until they are required, without deteriorating.*

BEETROOT

As well as the familiar round red beetroot, varieties may have white or yellow flesh and flattened, barrel or tapering shapes. Fast-maturing 'baby' beet and large maincrop storing varieties are available, although many can be used for both purposes.

Cultivation

Sow 2cm (¾in) deep in rows 23cm (9in) apart for early varieties, maincrops 30cm (12in) apart. Thin

▽ **A GOOD CROP OF BEETROOT** *will result if the seedlings are thinned at an early stage, up to 15cm (6in) apart for the largest roots, but less for 'baby beets'.*

to 10–15cm (4–6in) apart; alternatively space plants 15cm (6in) apart each way. Weed at first, then mulch with garden compost or grass clippings; water every two to three weeks in dry weather. Pull early roots when 5cm (2in) across. Lift maincrops in autumn, twisting off the foliage; store in dry sand or compost.

CARROTS

Varieties with small, sweet roots are useful for both early and successional sowings; large maincrop kinds for storing. Choose varieties according to the time of year crops are required.

Cultivation

Sow thinly, 1cm (½in) deep in rows 15cm (6in) apart, every two to three weeks from spring until midsummer. Keep moist but not waterlogged; weed carefully until seedlings have two or three true leaves, then mulch with compost or grass clippings. Thin several times to leave plants finally about 7.5cm (3in) apart. Pull as soon as large enough; maincrops may be over-wintered under straw on light soils, or dug in autumn and stored in dry sand.

PARSNIPS

These sweet winter roots are hardy and remain in the ground until they are

needed. Seeds have a limited lifespan and should be bought fresh each year.

Cultivation

Make a single sowing in spring, 1cm (½in) deep, in rows 30cm (12in) apart, either as pinches of seed 15cm (6in) apart or continuously; thin to leave single seedlings at this spacing. Water, weed and mulch as for carrots. Harvest roots as required from autumn onwards.

AVOIDING CARROT FLY

❖

- Hide carrot rows as intercrops among onions.

- Grow resistant varieties.

- Surround plants with a 45cm (18in) high screen of polythene or fleece.

- Avoid releasing the irresistible carrot scent by sowing sparsely to make thinning unnecessary; or soak plants thoroughly after thinning.

- Sow in mid-spring and midsummer when fly populations are lower.

POTATOES

Maincrop varieties are useful pioneers for new ground; early kinds occupy less space and yield welcome crops of new potatoes from early summer onwards.

Cultivation

Six weeks before planting, lay seed tubers in trays to 'chit' (produce short green sprouts). Starting in early spring, plant first earlies 10–15cm (4–6in) deep, every 30cm (12in), in rows 45–60cm (18–24in) apart; follow in mid-spring with other varieties, 38cm (15in) apart in rows 75cm (30in) apart. Earth up growing plants for frost

protection and to avoid green tubers. Water every two to three weeks. Start lifting earlies when the flowers first open, later kinds when the top growth turns brown. Store in boxes or paper sacks in a dark, frost-free place.

EARLY ROOT CROPS

For very early beetroot and carrots, sow in cell trays or modules under glass for planting out in spring after hardening off. Choose early varieties, round-rooted in the case of carrots, and sow a pinch

▷ **EARTH UP POTATO PLANTS** *by raking soil up into a neat ridge. Earth up all varieties in early summer when plants have made 20cm (8in) of growth, leaving the top 5cm (2in) exposed.*

△ **A HOME-MADE 'POGO'** *potato planter helps you make planting holes 10–15cm (4–5cm) deep.*

(six to eight carrot seeds, two or three beetroot capsules) in each cell. Germinate in warmth, then grow in a cooler place until large enough to plant out as unthinned clusters. Space a little further apart than usual.

TIPS FOR SUCCESS

BEETROOT

○ Soak seeds in water for an hour to improve germination.
○ Monogerm varieties reduce the need for thinning by producing a single plant.
○ Start sowing a month before the last frosts; repeat every 4 weeks until midsummer.
○ Small roots need 8–12 weeks to mature, maincrops 14–16 weeks.

CARROTS

○ Sow a fast-maturing variety in late winter or early spring under cover, and again in early autumn to extend the season.
○ Make early and late outdoor sowings in warm, sheltered positions.
○ Early varieties take 7–10 weeks to mature, maincrop 10–16 weeks.
○ On heavy or stony soils, grow round or short-rooted varieties.

PARSNIPS

○ Sow on a still day because seeds are papery and light.
○ Warm soils with a floating mulch if sowing before mid-spring.
○ Avoid hoeing too near the plants – damaged roots are prone to canker.
○ Mark rows with canes in autumn before the foliage dies down.

POTATOES

○ First earlies take 12–14 weeks to mature, second earlies 15–18 weeks, maincrops 18–22 weeks.
○ Always plant healthy tubers, certified disease-free.
○ Adding plenty of compost or well-rotted manure improves yields.
○ Choose varieties carefully: some are more resistant to pests, disease or drought than others.

27

The cabbage family

The brassica group is a varied race of leaf and stem vegetables, all enjoying rich, moist soil that is firm and alkaline. If these conditions are satisfied, you can be certain of high-quality crops all year round, especially in winter when other vegetables may be scarce.

CABBAGES

Round-headed or pointed, green or red, plain-leafed and savoy, there are cabbages to suit every taste; they are sown at various times of year according to their type. For garden use, choose fast-growing, compact varieties that stand for a long time without deterioration.

Cultivation

Sow 2.5cm (1in) deep where plants are to grow or in a nursery bed for transplanting; thin to 7.5cm (3in) apart. When about six weeks old transplant firmly to final positions in good light. Plants may also be raised in pots and modules under glass. Space spring

▼ **FOR THE BEST CROPS** *of solid Brussels sprouts, plants such as 'Oliver', shown here, need wide spacing in firm ground. Cover the plants with netting to foil hungry pigeons.*

CLUBROOT

❖

This root disease is perhaps the most serious ailment of brassicas. As a preventive, always lime the soil before planting any variety, and do not grow brassicas in the same place two years running. If you have clubroot, try growing plants in pots for as long as possible, so that they have a headstart when finally planted out.

---

cabbages 25cm (10in) apart each way, summer/autumn varieties 38–45cm (15–18in) apart and winter kinds 50cm (20in) each way. Keep the soil moist (mulching helps), and check regularly for pests such as caterpillars, aphids and whitefly; net against birds if necessary. Harvest as required, leaving 5–7.5cm (2–3in) stumps to resprout a further crop of small, leafy cabbages.

BRUSSELS SPROUTS

This hardy crop does not occupy much room if you choose a compact F1 hybrid and harvest the leafy plant tops when the lowest sprouts are just half-formed. Early, maincrop and late varieties extend the season from late summer to early spring.

Cultivation

Sow under glass in late winter or in a nursery bed outdoors in spring, 1cm

Cauliflower ready for harvesting

(½in) deep, and treat as for cabbages. Transplant finally when about 15cm (6in) high, 50–60cm (20–24in) apart each way and firm in. Feed at midsummer, but not afterwards, and support leaning stems with stakes. Start picking when lowest sprouts are large enough; remove leaves up to the level picked. In a cold winter, dig up complete stems and hang upside down under cover for picking.

CAULIFLOWERS

Cauliflowers are the greediest vegetable and a test of any gardener's skill: grow them in very well-manured soil and water regularly for best results. Green, yellow and red varieties are available, as well as the traditional white kinds and there is also a perennial form which makes a tall, branching bush.

Cultivation

Sow summer varieties in early spring, others a few weeks later, under glass or outdoors, as for Brussels sprouts. Water before and after transplanting to 45–60cm (18–24in) apart each way in rich, well-limed soil. Harvest while heads are still firm and tight; in cold weather

△ **RED- OR CURLY-LEAFED** *brassicas make an attractive contribution to decorative planting schemes.*

TIPS FOR SUCCESS

CABBAGES
- ○ F1 hybrids are often more uniform in size, with some pest or disease resistance.
- ○ If space is limited, concentrate on winter kinds, which are usually the most welcome.
- ○ Explore oriental brassicas for interesting shapes and flavours, but do not sow too early or they may bolt.

BRUSSELS SPROUTS
- ○ If space is short, transplant between rows of early potatoes.
- ○ Set young transplants with their lowest leaves at ground level.
- ○ Hard sprouts need very firm soil, so tread back any stems loosened by wind or frost.
- ○ The leafy tops are edible when picked as tasty 'greens'.

CAULIFLOWERS
- ○ In small gardens, grow mini-cauliflowers 15cm (6in) apart each way for individual servings.
- ○ Mulching helps keep the plants consistently moist.
- ○ Break some of the outer leaves to cover maturing heads and protect them from frost or sunshine.
- ○ Start cutting while heads are small, as crops often mature simultaneously.

BROCCOLI
- ○ Plants tolerate lower fertility than other brassicas, and are an easy alternative to cauliflowers.
- ○ The fastest varieties take 10–11 weeks to mature, others a month longer.
- ○ Choose a warm position for the earliest crops and provide light shade for summer sowings.
- ○ Sow an early variety in late summer and transplant to a cold frame for spring use.

29

dig up plants and hang upside down in a cool place for up to three weeks.

BROCCOLI

The spears of cauliflower-like florets make broccoli (calabrese) a popular crop, easily grown in the garden if you choose a fast-maturing F1 hybrid. Many produce secondary side shoots after the main head is cut.

Cultivation

Sow little and often in succession from early spring to midsummer. Sow in groups of two to three seeds in modules under glass or outdoors, 23cm (9in) apart each way to avoid any root disturbance; thin to a single seedling. Water regularly and mulch. Harvest the central head while still tight, feed with nitrogenous fertilizer and cut resulting side shoots when 10cm (4in) long.

PURPLE AND WHITE SPROUTING BROCCOLI

❖

These popular brassicas provide succulent pickings of white or purple flower buds early in the year. Sow in a nursery bed in spring for transplanting in summer 45–60cm (18–24in) apart. The young shoots start forming in late winter and may be cut over a long season.

More leaf crops

There are probably more edible leaf crops than any other type of vegetable. Nearly half of these are brassicas, a constantly evolving group as more varieties are steadily introduced. But there are many further leaf crops to explore, including spinach and its alternatives, all of them highly nutritious, and many with outstanding decorative value too.

ORIENTAL BRASSICAS

Most oriental brassicas have a distinctive delicate flavour quite different from that of European cabbages. Unlike the latter, they are not vegetables for boiling until soft, but should be stir-fried, lightly steamed or even eaten raw while they are still young. Chinese cabbages come in a variety of shapes, some round or cylindrical, others conical or loose-leafed. Chinese and Japanese greens are often aromatic or spicy, and again need brief cooking only. They are all suitable for autumn and winter use, and in cooler gardens may be grown all year, especially if modern fast-growing hybrid varieties are chosen.

Cultivation

Most varieties are sown from mid-summer to early autumn, in situ or in modules to avoid root disturbance, which can cause bolting. Thin or transplant at 23–30cm (9–12in) spacings in rich, moisture-retentive alkaline soil. Water and mulch in dry weather. You can also sow in spring, thinning seedlings 5–8cm (2–3in) apart for cutting as seedling crops when about 10cm (4in) high.

KALE

The extended family of kales is very diverse, ranging from the almost agricultural marrow-stem and thousand-headed kales to the smaller and more palatable plain-leafed borecole and ornamental curly kales. Tuscan black cabbage, otherwise called Cavolo Nero or Nero di Toscana, has long, curiously blistered leaves, while Abyssinian cabbage (often sold as texsel greens) is a fast-growing miniature form. All types of kale are hardy, precocious plants with prolific crops of tender young shoots that are best steamed or stir-fried.

Cultivation

Sow outdoors in a nursery bed in late spring and transplant 45cm (18in) apart each way about 6 weeks later, when plants have 4–6 leaves. Use the space between for catch-crops of radishes or lettuces. Small main leaves can be picked from late autumn, but the true crop appears from late winter onwards as young leafy sideshoots develop – cut these when they are about 10cm (4in) long.

ORNAMENTAL LEAF CROPS

Years ago dwarf curly kale was a popular foliage plant grown for its impact in mass winter and spring bedding. Chard is used for the same purpose in summer, especially red-stemmed varieties and mixtures of red, pink, gold and white kinds. Traditional beetroot varieties with rich red or purple leaves add opulence to borders, and blend well with oriental brassicas such as frilly mizuna, purple-ribbed choy sum and tatsoi (pak choi) with its immaculate heads of spoon-shaped leaves.

Chinese Cabbage 'Ruffles'

Swiss chard

SPINACH

Summer spinach is not an easy crop to grow unless you can provide rich moist soil, with some shade from hot sunshine to avoid early bolting to seed. Winter spinach crops from late autumn until spring, and is not so fussy. Some modern varieties may be grown at both seasons.

Cultivation

Sow summer varieties where they are to grow, at intervals between early spring and early summer, and thin to 15–20cm (6–8in) apart; winter kinds are sown in situ in late summer or early autumn, and thinned to 23cm (9in) apart. Keep watered in dry weather, and cover winter varieties from mid-autumn. Pick regularly, especially summer crops which might otherwise start flowering.

SPINACH BEET AND CHARD

These are more productive alternatives to true spinach. Spinach beet (leaf beet or perpetual spinach) has large, fleshy leaves with a mild flavour and a long season of use – two

Spinach 'Cruciferae'

> ### OTHER KINDS OF SPINACH
> ❖
> New Zealand spinach (*Tetragonia expansa*) is a tender, prostrate annual with sprawling stems of rich green succulent foliage that makes good ground cover and defies heat or drought more successfully than other spinaches. The young leaves of 'good king henry' (*Chenopodium bonus-henricus*) are used as spinach, while its new spring shoots are an asparagus substitute – it is a robust perennial and prolific self-seeder. Heat-loving Malabar spinach (*Basella alba*) and hardy annual orach or mountain spinach (*Atriplex hortensis*), especially in its red and gold forms, are other flavoursome crops worth sampling.

---

sowings will supply pickings all year. Swiss chard, silver chard or seakale beet is an eye-catching crop with broad white or coloured ribs and succulent, deeply savoyed leaves: the midribs and leaf blades are often treated as two different vegetables.

Cultivation

Sow both crops in full sun or light shade, in spring for summer and autumn use, in late summer for winter and spring. Transplant from a nursery bed or thin sowings in situ to 30cm (12in) apart. Water in dry weather and mulch light soils. Harvest leaves when large enough or cut whole plants, leaving 2.5cm (1in) high stumps for regrowth.

TIPS FOR SUCCESS

ORIENTAL BRASSICAS
○ For an economical way to grow the full range, prick out mixed oriental saladini seedlings and grow plants on to full size.
○ In hot gardens, choose bolt-resistant varieties and do not sow before midsummer.
○ Chinese cabbage stumps 2.5–5cm (1–2in) high left in the ground will often resprout if they are fed and watered well.

KALE
○ A late winter sowing of curly kale, thinned to 5cm (2in) apart, produces a fast crop of tender greens for stir-frying.
○ In a cool position, new shoots will continue appearing up to early summer if prevented from flowering.
○ Kale is less disease-prone than other brassicas, and makes a good choice where clubroot may be present.

SPINACH
○ For late sowings, choose a variety resistant to mildew.
○ Spread picking over several plants, rather than stripping one or two completely.
○ Winter spinach thrives best with very good drainage and protection from mid-autumn to early spring.

SPINACH BEET AND CHARD
○ Sow in a deep box or frame in autumn, leave unthinned, and cut baby leaves for salads.
○ Mulching helps conserve moisture for these thirsty crops, and improves their quality.
○ Lime acid soils to improve plant vigour and leaf colour.

31

Extending the choice

There is no end to the range of vegetables you can try. Apart from the main salad, cabbage, root, and pea and bean groups, several other important crops deserve consideration if you decide to expand the variety of fresh produce you grow.

△ **RAISE MARROWS** *from seed in small, individual pots under glass. Made from newspaper, these pots are degradable in soil.*

BULBING ONIONS

An essential vegetable for any kitchen and easily grown if you plant sets (immature bulbs already several weeks old). They tolerate poor soil, give a flying start to the season and often mature earlier than plants from seed.

Cultivation

Choose a site manured for a previous crop, or fork in plenty of compost and firm well. Plant sets with a trowel, every 7.5–10cm (3–4in) in rows 25–30cm (10–12in) apart, leaving their tips at soil level; start maincrop sets in early spring, over-wintered kinds in mid-autumn.

Weed regularly (take care when hoeing as their roots are very shallow), water in dry weather and feed at monthly intervals. Start harvesting when bulbs are large enough. For storing, wait until tops die down, fork up and spread in the sun to dry; keep in a cool, frost-free place.

◁ **A POPULAR AND HARDY** *member of the onion family, leeks are undemanding plants that may be tucked in wherever there is space. Their foliage casts little shade over nearby plants.*

GARLIC

An increasingly popular vegetable, garlic is very hardy and trouble-free to grow. Start in autumn because plants need several weeks at low temperatures if they are to make good bulbs.

Cultivation

Prepare the ground as for bulbing onions. Separate bulbs into cloves, and plant single cloves, point upwards, 15–20cm (6–8in) apart each way in holes 7.5cm (3in) deep. Alternatively, pot bulbs up individually and keep in a cold frame until they can be transplanted in spring. Water in dry weather and keep weed-free. When the leaf tips turn yellow, fork up bulbs and suspend or spread out to dry in the sun. Store in a frost-free, dry place.

LEEKS

Whether grown as fat, short-stemmed plants or pencil-slim mini-leeks, this undemanding crop can be available for up to eight months of the year. There are early, mid-season and late varieties, although their seasons of use overlap.

Cultivation

Buy plants in early summer, or sow in a nursery bed outdoors in spring, 1–2cm (½–¾in) deep, and thin seedlings to 4cm (1½in) apart. Plant out when about 15–23cm (6–8in) high with two or three strong leaves, spacing them every 15cm (6in) in rows 30cm (12in) apart.

△ **DRY GARLIC** *and maincrop onions thoroughly, then store bulbs in an airy place to keep them sound for as long as possible.*

Either plant on the surface, or for a longer blanch make holes 15cm (6in) deep with a dibber and drop a seedling in each; fill the hole with water to settle plants. Water if dry and feed once or twice up to late summer. Harvest as soon as they reach a usable size.

MARROWS AND COURGETTES

The squash family also embraces other summer kinds such as custard and spaghetti squash, and winter types that include pumpkins and edible gourds for storing. All are grown in the same way as marrows and courgettes.

Cultivation

Plants are not hardy, so start them in pots under glass a month before planting out. Sow seeds on edge, singly, 2.5cm (1in) deep in small pots. Dig a hole for each plant, 30cm (12in) deep and wide, and half-fill with decayed manure or garden compost; top up with soil, leaving a depression for watering. After the last frosts, plant in the centre of the depression. Water lavishly every week when flowering starts, and mulch to conserve soil moisture. Pinch out tips of trailing

△ **LEEKS HAVE BEEN GROWN** *through a mulch of newspaper. A light mulch will also keep onions moist, but the bulbs should be exposed to sunlight as soon as they ripen.*

varieties when about 60cm (24in) long. Start to gather courgettes when about 10cm (4in) long with the flower still attached; cut other squash when large enough.

△ **GOLD COURGETTES** *are as tasty as the more familiar green varieties and make an ideal crop for home cultivation.*

STORING SQUASHES
❖

Harvest pumpkins and other winter kinds before the autumn frosts, ideally when their stems start to dry out. Cut each fruit with a long piece of stem, and cure the skin for two weeks in warm sunshine, outdoors or under glass; when the skin is hard and sounds hollow if tapped, the squash is ready to store, on a shelf or suspended in netting in a warm, airy place.

TIPS FOR SUCCESS

ONIONS
○ Watering or feeding maincrop onions after midsummer may shorten their storage life.
○ Use split, thick-necked and flowering bulbs first as these do not keep well.
○ Some gardeners alternate rows of onions and carrots to confuse invading carrot root fly.

GARLIC
○ Garlic prefers light soil, so work plenty of grit into heavy ground.
○ Plants often flower, but this does not affect their storage life.
○ Viruses can cause yellow leaf markings: infected bulbs are still safe to eat, however.
○ Save bulbs from a healthy crop for replanting the following year.

LEEKS
○ Sow earlier crops in late winter, under glass in trays or modules.
○ For a longer blanch, draw soil up the stems as they develop.
○ Early varieties are not hardy and should be used before winter.

MARROWS AND COURGETTES
○ Grow trailing marrows under sweetcorn plants for ground cover.
○ Marrows and pumpkins planted on the top of completed compost heaps revel in the extra fertility.
○ Increase marrow yields by cutting smaller fruits for immediate use, leaving the last few to ripen for storing.
○ Tying courgette stems to vertical stakes as they grow improves air circulation and reduces mildew.

33

Exploring unusual crops

Kitchen gardening becomes compulsive, and you might be tempted to try unusual personal favourites or old-fashioned crops rarely seen in modern gardens. Some familiar vegetables have additional virtues only revealed to gardeners – juicy green turnip 'tops', for example, or crisp salsify flower buds are but a sampler of the wider field.

Globe artichoke

TURNIPS

Good quality swedes need a long growing season in rich soil, but yellow turnip varieties take less time, will tolerate dryer conditions and make perfectly acceptable substitutes. Early white or purple-topped turnips are a gourmet vegetable to grow fast as a catch-crop in moist soils and harvest while still small.

Cultivation

Sow early turnip varieties in situ, every 3–4 weeks from early spring until midsummer, and thin seedlings to 8–10cm (3–4in) apart; in early autumn sow a hardy type to cut as 'greens' in spring when 15cm (6in) high. Keep well watered, and do not leave roots to get large and fibrous.

CELERIAC

This close relative of celery develops a firm, swollen stem at ground level, and is harvested in autumn for use as a raw or cooked vegetable; the young leaves may also be used for flavouring. Celeriac succeeds where soils are too dry or seasons too hot for celery to grow well, although rich, moist conditions produce the best 'bulbs'.

Cultivation

Sow and plant as for celery, spacing transplants 30cm (12in) apart each way. Water well in dry weather, and mulch. Feed occasionally for the largest bulbs. Dig up in mid-autumn; store in boxes of straw, or cover with leaves, straw or soil outdoors for frost-protection.

JERUSALEM ARTICHOKES

The sweet tubers of this sunflower relative are rarely sold in shops, because they shrivel quickly on exposure to air. Easily grown and very nutritious, they are a starch-free substitute for potatoes. The tall-stemmed plants make excellent seasonal screens and windbreaks.

Cultivation

Plant small tubers in early spring, 10cm (4in) deep and 30cm (12in) apart. Water and mulch in dry weather, and earth up or support stems in exposed positions. Harvest from early autumn onwards, as required, or dig up the whole crop, save small tubers for replanting and store the rest buried in boxes of moist sand.

◁ CELERIAC STARTS TO
fatten its bulbs at soil level once the summer extends into autumn.

GLOBE ARTICHOKES

These aristocratic perennials need a permanent sheltered site. With their handsome blue-green leaves and mauve thistle-like flowers, they deserve space in a herbaceous border, although they appreciate more compost or manure than is usually allocated to flowers. The fat green or purple flower buds are the part eaten, either fresh or bottled for winter use.

Cultivation

Sow in a nursery bed in early spring, and transplant the strongest seedlings 60–75cm (24–30in) apart in summer in a warm, sunny position, or plant rooted offsets at this spacing in spring. Water regularly and mulch with compost or manure. Cut the small lateral buds first, in midsummer, followed by the large central head. Divide every 3–4 years, replanting young offsets in fresh soil.

SALSIFY

A traditional vegetable with mildly flavoured white roots and attractive mauve flowers; scorzonera is a yellow-flowered relative with black-skinned roots. Both are easy to grow and trouble-free. Scorzonera is a perennial that would embellish any flower border, while salsify can be left in and earthed

34

up over winter to force and blanch the tender new leaf shoots.

Cultivation

Sow in mid-spring where plants are to grow, in full sun and well-broken soil. Thin the seedlings to 10–15cm (4–6in) apart, and keep moist for the heaviest roots. Dig up as required from mid-autumn; on heavy soils, lift the whole crop and store in boxes of dry sand in a cool place.

ASPARAGUS

Although this delicious perennial fern is harvested for just 8 weeks, leading up to the longest day, the graceful foliage is a decorative asset all season, until mid-autumn when it turns bright yellow as it dies down. There is no need for a large

◁ **SCORZONERA** *has a black skin under which lies a tender white root with a delicious subtle flavour.*

traditional bed: asparagus thrives in small groups, single rows or even in large deep containers.

Cultivation

Sow in late spring outdoors, thin to 8cm (3in) apart and transplant the best seedlings 45cm (18in) apart a year later; or buy 1- or 2-year old crowns and plant them 10cm (4in) deep with their roots spread out. Mulch annually with compost or decayed manure after cutting down the dead fronds in autumn. Harvest nothing the first summer, just a few spears the following season, and start full cropping the year after that.

SWEET FENNEL

Sometimes known as Florence fennel, this late crop has feathery foliage similar to the herb fennel, and a crisp, swollen 'bulb' at the base of its leafy stem. Rich soil and warmth are essential – try growing a few plants as a feature in a large container that can be moved into the sun or under cover according to the vagaries of the weather.

Cultivation

Sow in summer, in situ or in modules to avoid root disturbance, and thin or transplant 30cm (12in) apart. Keep consistently moist; feed occasionally. Earth up the stem base when it starts to swell and blanch for 2–3 weeks. Harvest from early autumn onwards.

CARDOONS

❖

These cousins of globe artichokes are even more decorative, with magnificent blue-grey foliage and towering stems if allowed to flower. Grow single specimens in prominent positions as garden highlights. Blanch the leaf stems for 4–6 weeks before use by tying the leaves in a loose bundle and wrapping them in brown paper or a straw jacket.

TIPS FOR SUCCESS

TURNIPS
○ Roots left in the ground over winter can be ridged over with soil to force tender blanched shoots in spring.
○ Sow early turnips and carrots in a frame in late winter, in alternate rows, and interplant with lettuces.

CELERIAC
○ Remove some lower leaves in late summer to expose bulbs to sunlight.
○ Crops survive until late spring, so dig up and heel in elsewhere if you need the space for cultivation.

JERUSALEM ARTICHOKES
○ Tubers left in will grow again, but annual re-planting in fresh rich soil gives the best crops.
○ Cut and dry stems in autumn for plant supports the following year.

GLOBE ARTICHOKES
○ For the largest heads, thin branching inflorescence to leave 3–4 buds.
○ Choose purple varieties for the best flavour, and cover less spiny kinds with a winter mulch of leaves or straw.

SALSIFY
○ Plants are biennial, producing edible flower buds in their second year.
○ Dead-head flowering plants to prevent prolific self-seeding.

ASPARAGUS
○ Hybrid varieties produce fat, all-male shoots, but need more lavish feeding.
○ Clear all perennial weeds before planting, as they are difficult to remove later.

SWEET FENNEL
○ Some modern bolt-resistant varieties can be sown from late spring; other-wise, wait until after the longest day.
○ When harvesting, leave a 2.5cm (1in) stump to produce small, tender shoots for flavouring.

35

Greenhouses and cold frames

Confining your plans to crops that will grow outdoors unprotected leaves you at the mercy of fickle weather conditions. Installing a greenhouse or cold frame can reduce this annual gamble and allow you to extend your repertoire of crops.

CHOOSING A GREENHOUSE

A greenhouse is a major investment but will earn its keep many times over, allowing seedlings to be raised earlier than normal, sheltering over-wintered plants and offering a warm microclimate for sensitive summer crops. There are models to suit every pocket and site, and you will need to decide your needs and priorities carefully before buying. A lean-to structure or conservatory occupies less space than a freestanding house and benefits from the reflected warmth of its supporting wall. An aluminium house glazed to ground level lets in plenty of light but will be colder in winter than a timber model with solid sides to waist level. While not as efficient as a greenhouse, a polytunnel provides inexpensive year-round protection and may be a safer option than glass where there are children.

▷ **A GREENHOUSE** *of any size provides a sanctuary for young seedlings and cold-sensitive plants.*

Whichever type you decide on, always choose the largest practical size – you will soon fill it, especially in a cold spring when many different crops are sown or may be waiting to go outside.

GREENHOUSE MANAGEMENT

Plants under glass are completely dependent on you for their welfare. They might survive inattention for a week or more in winter, but their needs during the growing season usually demand daily commitment. Make a point of checking every morning or evening – you will soon learn to recognize the distinctive moist,

◁ **A POLYTUNNEL** *is cheaper than a greenhouse and easier to erect, but it raises temperatures effectively and extends the growing season.*

buoyant smell of a well-regulated greenhouse when you open the door.

Ventilation is important at all times. Even on a cold day, opening a vent for an hour at noon will help disperse stale air, while you might need to leave windows and doors wide open at night in midsummer. Temperatures under glass can soar or plummet dramatically, but shading the glass between spring and autumn, and lining the inside with insulation in winter helps avoid these extremes. Damping down – lightly watering or spraying the floor and staging – also cools the air in summer, but keep plants as dry as possible in winter to discourage fungal diseases. After watering, leave the can full so that its contents adjust to the indoor temperature and you can save time if you notice a plant in distress.

GREENHOUSE EQUIPMENT

❖

STAGING You will need some form of staging to keep plants at a comfortable working height. Collapsible staging is the most versatile and may be erected temporarily over a soil border to provide for all kinds of crops. Slatted tops allow good drainage and air circulation; solid panels can be covered with gravel or capillary matting to reduce watering.

HEATING Any form of heating is expensive and needs to be justified. The best arrangement is to insulate the whole house, and just heat a small area during a hard frost or when sowing in spring. A portable paraffin heater is the most economical for emergency use.

AUTOMATIC VENTILATION This is almost essential if you are to avoid sudden surges in heat and a lot of worry at critical times. Fit a thermostatically controlled opener (*see inset*) on each vent, and adjust them to suit the temperature regime.

AUTOMATIC IRRIGATION A more sophisticated aid, particularly useful for sensitive plants or if you cannot check frequently in summer. Water is supplied from a small reservoir or from the mains via a timed control.

PROPAGATOR This is useful for sowing and rooting cuttings in heat. You can buy thermostatically controlled electric models, or a simple plastic and timber case will provide enough extra local heat.

USING A COLD FRAME

A cold frame is basically a solid, glazed or plastic-clad box with an adjustable lid. Although not always so congenial a working environment for the gardener, a frame can be as versatile as a greenhouse, especially if it is portable. The best kind has no fixed base, so that you can sow or plant direct into the soil inside and then move the frame to a new site when the contents no longer need protection. A positive advantage of a frame is that you can open or remove the lid to admit rain and thus save the need for watering, and it is also easy to insulate in winter with sheets of fleece or bubble plastic or an old blanket.

A frame offers a controlled environment for a whole range of activities such as covering early sowings or late cuttings in a nursery bed, cosseting cold-sensitive summer crops such as melons or bush tomatoes, drying onions in a wet summer and maintaining winter salads in peak condition. You can even stand it on a fermenting compost heap to trap the high temperatures like a hot-bed, for forcing out of season crops. There need never be a time when the frame is empty.

◁ *A COLD FRAME is inexpensive, compact and infinitely versatile; many gardeners consider it more essential than a greenhouse.*

A GREENHOUSE YEAR

WINTER
Save heat by insulating the structure, and if necessary cover plants with fleece or newspapers for extra frost protection. Maintain a dry atmosphere, but lightly water any growing plants and ventilate occasionally on mild days. Clear dead or diseased leaves and exhausted winter crops before they can set up fungal infections. Early in the season, chit potatoes (see page 27); sow carrots and other early crops in the soil; force strawberries and mint. Later, start the first sowings in pots and trays.

SPRING
Retain insulation as long as necessary. Wash the glass for maximum light, and towards late spring apply some shading. Ventilate on warm days but shut down by mid-afternoon. Increase watering as plant growth revives. Prick out early seedlings and keep up sowing as the days lengthen. Avoid congestion by moving larger plants to the cold frame in good time. Plant tomatoes and other summer crops by the end of the season.

SUMMER
Fully shade the glass and protect young seedlings from sun scorch with newspaper. Ventilate freely, check the watering at least once a day and damp down in hot weather. Take precautions against greenhouse pests. Feed, train and pollinate summer crops.

AUTUMN
As temperatures drop and growth subsides, stop damping down and reduce watering gradually. Ventilate on mild days, but beware cold nights; check heating and insulation. Clean off shading, wash the glass, and fumigate against pests. Clear summer crops as they finish, and sow winter vegetables in trays or in the soil. Take late cuttings and pot up herbs for winter supplies.

37

Greenhouse crops

Protection against the elements, especially early and late frosts, helps ensure success with crops that need more warmth than might be available outdoors. Under glass, crops such as dwarf French beans, winter lettuces and strawberries can be raised to maturity out of season. In the summer, four cold-sensitive vegetables are particular favourites for growing bags, pots and greenhouse borders: these are tomatoes, cucumbers, peppers and aubergines.

Plum tomatoes 'Super Roma'

TOMATOES

Although many varieties of tomato may be grown outdoors in a good year, early heavy yields are more predictable under glass. Choose an indoor variety described as short-jointed to ensure the maximum number of fruit trusses in a limited space.

Cultivation

Plants may be bought or started from seed, sowing them at about 18°C (65°F) in midwinter for growing with heat, and in early spring for unheated greenhouses. Sow thinly in pots and just cover with compost for pricking out later, or sow two seeds in a 7.5cm (3in) pot and remove the weaker seedling. Keep warm and evenly moist, and pot on if necessary. Plant out tomatoes when the first cluster of flower buds is visible. Water and feed regularly, remove the side shoots from tall (cordon or indeterminate) varieties, and support on canes or strings. Pinch out growing tips two leaves beyond the fourth or fifth flower truss. Harvest fruits when fully coloured, removing lower yellow leaves at the same time. Clear out the old stems at the end of the season.

CUCUMBERS

Indoor varieties of cucumber need high temperatures and humidity to produce their heavy crops of slim, tender fruits. All-female types are easiest to grow, because others need daily checking to remove male flowers and so prevent fertilization (this results in a bitter flavour).

▷ CUCUMBERS grown under glass can produce heavy yields.

Cultivation

Buy plants in late spring or sow seeds individually in early spring, 1cm (½in) deep in 7.5cm (3in) pots and germinate at 26°C (80°F). Move on into 11cm (4¼in) pots and provide a thin cane

◁ WITH THEIR EXTENSIVE root system, tomato plants need to be grown in tubs or generous-sized pots to ensure maximum yields.

POPULAR GROWING METHODS UNDER GLASS

❖

POTS: 23cm (9in) is the smallest practical size of container; use a rich, soil-based compost (for example, John Innes No 3).

GROWING BAGS: Plant two or three tomato or cucumber plants (three of peppers or aubergines) in each bag. For heavier crops use two growing bags, one sitting above the other, with the plastic cut out underneath each plant to encourage deeper rooting.

SOIL BORDERS: Dig in plenty of well-rotted compost or decayed manure before planting, and change or sterilize the soil each year to prevent the spread of infection from one crop to the next.

TRAINING PLANTS

❖

Tie cucumbers or cordon varieties of tomato to upright canes or gently twist their stems around strings suspended from the greenhouse roof. If you have only a few plants, space them out and allow two low side shoots to grow, one on each side, to form further stems that can be trained at an angle from the main plant. Bush tomatoes need no training; use short twigs or canes to support laden branches.

for training the main shoot. Keep warm and in a moist atmosphere. When plants have 8–10 leaves, plant out and train upwards as for tomatoes. Feed every two weeks and pinch out the growing tip when the main shoot reaches the roof; pinch out side shoots two leaves beyond a female flower (look for the tiny cucumber at its base). Cut fruits as soon as they are large enough.

PEPPERS

Both sweet and hot chilli peppers can be grown in the same conditions as for tomatoes, trained on canes or wires to keep them tidy. Surplus fruits can be dried in warmth for winter use.

Cultivation

Buy plants in late spring or sow in early spring in the same way as for tomatoes,

Aubergine 'Asian Bride'

in a temperature of 20–25°C (68–77°F); grow the seedlings on at 12–15°C (54–60°F). Pot on as necessary in soil-based compost. Plant in late spring, and water and feed with tomato fertilizer regularly. Tie main stems to canes or strings, pinching out the growing tips of sweet peppers when about 38cm (15in) high; chilli peppers can be trained as cordons up to about 1.5m (5ft). Gather fruits when they are fully coloured.

AUBERGINES

A popular crop with heavy, waxy, highly ornamental fruits that may be purple, white or maroon/white striped. Grow several plants because each will set only four to five full-sized fruits.

Cultivation

Grow as for peppers, keeping the seedlings at 15–18°C (60–65°F). Plant in mid- or late spring, support plants with canes and pinch out the growing tip when about 30cm (12in) high. Dampen down the greenhouse regularly during flowering, and when five fruits have formed, remove any further side shoots and flowers. Feed with tomato fertilizer every time you water. Harvest fruit when fully coloured and still shiny.

TIPS FOR SUCCESS

TOMATOES
- Too much water or fertilizer and too little sunshine can all dilute the flavour of the fruit.
- Always use a tomato or high-potash fertilizer as excessive nitrogen produces leaves rather than fruit.
- Check regularly for pests such as aphids, whitefly and red spider mite.
- Help flowers to set fruit by tapping the supporting canes or strings and damping the surroundings on a warm, sunny day.
- Ripen green fruits at the end of the season by spreading them in a box with a ripe apple or banana.

CUCUMBERS
- When planting in a border, set plants on a mound of soil for good drainage.
- Cucumbers need much more humidity than tomatoes, so keep them apart in the same greenhouse.
- Make sure no fruits are overlooked and left to turn yellow, as cropping may then cease.
- Use clean compost, pots and labels to avoid fungal diseases, and ventilate in hot weather.

PEPPERS
- Watch out for aphids, whitefly and red spider mites: spray as necessary.
- Harvesting sweet peppers while still green encourages the production of more fruits and a higher overall yield.

AUBERGINES
- Start plants earlier than peppers if possible, because crops take five months to mature.
- Protect young plants against fluctuations in temperature, especially on cool nights.

39

Saving space with mini-vegetables

Fist-size cauliflowers and carrots no larger than a little finger are part of a revolution in attitudes to food crops. The emphasis is changing from monster crops to compact varieties planted close together so that a tiny patch can yield a whole range of fresh, more delicately-flavoured, miniature vegetables.

△ **COMPARED TO** *demanding, full-sized cauliflower plants, mini-varieties produce firm, individual portions from a small plot.*

THINK SMALL

The basic methods of cultivation are the same as for normal vegetables, with one essential difference: compact growing varieties are planted closer together, giving a high density of small plants that are harvested while still young. Many mature faster than their larger relatives, which permits a quick turnover of vegetables and the chance to grow more in succession. This method is ideally suited to cultivation in small beds, with plants arranged in compact groups to produce a patchwork of varied crops at different stages of maturity.

THE GROUNDWORK

The total yield from a small plot managed in this way over the whole season is quite large, so fertile soil is essential. Work in plenty of garden compost, well-rotted manure or a proprietary concentrated manure when preparing the ground at the start of the season, and again after

40

MINI-PLANTS AND MINI-PRODUCE

❖

It is important to distinguish between normal varieties (for example, leeks) that tolerate close spacings, yielding smaller produce but taking the usual time to mature, and mini-vegetables (some lettuces, turnips and dwarf kale), bred to make small plants at high density, often maturing earlier. There are also baby varieties that are grown in the normal way but yield miniature produce: baby sweetcorn, tiny Brussels sprouts and small-seeded broad beans are popular examples.

◁ **WITH THEIR NATURALLY** *compact and upright habit, small cos lettuce varieties such as 'Little Gem' are the perfect option for high-density planting schemes.*

GUIDE TO SPACING AND RATE OF GROWTH

VARIETY	SPACING (within rows)	SPACING (between rows)	TIME TO MATURITY	SIZE AT MATURITY
Beetroot 'Pronto'	2.5cm (1in)	15cm (6in).	12 weeks	5cm (2in) across
Cabbage 'Minicole','Protovoy' (savoy)	15cm (6in)	15cm (6in)	12–20 weeks	from 8cm (3in) across
Calabrese 'Trixie'	15cm (6in)	15cm (6in)	10–12 weeks	8–10cm (3–4in) diam.
Carrot, Amsterdam or Nantes type	1cm (½in)	15cm (6in)	10–12 weeks	finger-thickness
Cauliflower 'Dominant', 'Idol'	13cm (5in)	15cm (6in)	15 weeks	8cm (3in) diam.
Kale 'Showbor'	15cm (6in)	15cm (6in)	14–16 weeks	30cm (12in) high
Kohl Rabi 'Logo'	2.5cm (1in)	15cm (6in)	10 weeks	4–5cm (1½–2in) across
Leek 'King Richard'	1cm (½in)	15cm (6in)	12–14 weeks	2cm (¾in) thick
Lettuce 'Little Gem', 'Tom Thumb'	15cm (6in)	15cm (6in)	8–12 weeks	15cm (6in) diam.
Parsnip 'Gladiator'	8cm (3in)	15cm (6in)	20 weeks	2.5–5cm (1–2in) thick
Potato 'Rocket', 'Swift'	25cm (10in)	25cm (10in)	12 weeks	5cm (2in) across
Turnip 'Tokyo Cross'	2.5cm (1in)	15cm (6in)	7–8 weeks	2.5–5cm (1–2in) across

41

clearing one crop to make way for the next. No extra fertilizer should be necessary, but a compost mulch round young plants helps sustain fast growth and can be forked in between crops to improve soil fertility and structure.

THE PLAN
Start early by making the first sowings under glass in pots or modules, cluster-sown where appropriate, and planting these out under cloches or fleece. At planting time start another batch in the same way for succession; this ensures that the ground is never empty, because there is always another sowing waiting to follow on. Plant or sow (crops such as parsnips must be sown direct) in rows or blocks at close spacings (*see box above*), siting similar-sized crops next to each other so that none competes unfairly for light. Keep the ground evenly moist to promote the fast, consistent growth essential for success.

WHICH VEGETABLES?
Many normal varieties can be grown closer together than usual to give smaller produce: maincrop onions produce medium-sized bulbs at 4cm (1½in) apart, for example; early potatoes can be spaced as close as 25cm (10in) apart each way; and slender types of carrot grow happily 5cm (2in) apart each way. Special varieties have also been developed that are naturally small at maturity and these are often the best choice where space is limited or only a few vegetables are needed. When harvesting any variety, start by using every alternate plant, leaving the others to continue growing.

△ **ROUND CARROT** *varieties may be sown and grown in clusters and quickly produce juicy, bite-sized roots at close spacing.*

Productive containers

High-quality produce can be harvested fresh from a backyard, a terrace or a balcony – indeed, anywhere there is no open ground – if you grow your crops in pots. From apple trees and runner beans in half-barrels to small strawberry pots and parsley pigs, container cultivation adds a decorative element to the garden as well as yielding satisfying rewards.

VEGETABLES

Most vegetable crops may be grown in pots, including early potatoes forced out of season or runner beans trained on a wigwam of canes and surrounded with yellow courgettes. Cucumbers, peppers and tomatoes all crop well in 30cm (12in) pots stood against a warm wall, especially if you plunge the base of the pots in a growing bag for extra rooting volume – in this way a row of tomatoes can be arranged along the side of greenhouse or shed.

BUSH AND TREE FRUIT

In a large container, 38cm (15in) or more, decoratively trained fruit such as standard gooseberries or a weeping apple can make impressive features for a permanent position. Top fruits must be grafted onto very dwarfing rootstocks to limit their growth, although there are genetically dwarf varieties of peaches and other fruits; it is even possible to assemble a mini-orchard of cordon or columnar apples in pots. Fig trees have vigorous roots that support excessive leaf growth

△ **ALPINE STRAWBERRIES**, *with their trailing growth and decorative appearance, can be as effective as summer bedding for a trough or box.*

unless restrained, and these crop well in a half-barrel or large planter.

BASIC CULTIVATION
Choosing containers

A pot must be the right size for the plant. Some short-term crops, such as basil or leaf lettuce, can remain in 13–15cm (5–6in) pots throughout their growth, whereas other plants need more

◁ **PROVIDED SUPPORT** *is given, tall plants such as runner beans or tomatoes can be grown in large, heavy containers filled with soil-based compost for stability.*

BLUEBERRIES IN POTS

❖

Blueberries (*Vaccinium* spp.) hate lime in the soil, and must be grown in containers if the soil is not naturally acid. They are attractive bushes, often turning fiery shades of copper and orange in autumn. Plant each bush (you will need at least two for cross-pollination) in a tub of ericaceous or lime-free compost and water regularly with rainwater in summer. Net plants against birds as soon as the fruit starts ripening in late summer. Thin some of the older stems from mature bushes in winter and shear lightly to shape in spring.

 THE AMOUNT OF *compost in a growing bag is limited, so start plants off in large pots and stand one bag on top of another to increase the rooting volume.*

container. Cover the bottom with a generous drainage layer (pebbles, broken clay pots or crushed stones), and use a good potting compost, preferably soil-based for stability; this may be mixed with some garden soil if it is clean and fertile. Stand all containers where plants receive optimum light, warmth and shelter, bearing in mind that pots are portable features and can be moved according to the season and the maturity of the contents. Growing

tender plants in containers allows you to move them around to follow the sun or to avoid frost, as was traditional with citrus fruits kept in large, square Versailles boxes.

When grown in pots, plants need more frequent watering and you should check them regularly – daily watering will be required in hot weather but less often in shade or winter. A month or so after potting, start feeding every week with a dilute, balanced fertilizer and turn containers occasionally to encourage even growth.

room as they develop: remember that undersized pots cramp growth, while roots in too large a pot can rot in a quantity of stagnant soil. Ornamental pots such as strawberry towers may be adapted for other crops, such as leaf lettuces or a collection of thymes. Generous-sized containers, such as half-barrels and tubs, will accommodate a variety of larger vegetables and also trained fruits (on dwarfing rootstocks where appropriate). Make sure that all containers have adequate drainage holes in the bottom.

Good growing habits

After buying a potted plant, gently knock it out of the container: if its roots are winding around the rootball, pot it on straight into the next size of

▷ FIGS CROP *more heavily if their roots are restricted in a pot. Container cultivation also allows figs to be moved indoors in a cold winter.*

EARLY STRAWBERRIES

— ❖ —

Perpetual strawberry varieties in pots can be forced into an early harvest in a warm, sheltered place, with a later crop following outdoors in the autumn. Pot up rooted runners in 9cm (3½in) pots in summer and keep outdoors, potting them on as they develop, either individually into 13cm (5in) pots or several plants together in towers or stacking pots to save space. In late winter, bring under glass to force early blooms; after fruiting, move outdoors and feed to encourage an autumn crop.

43

Growing soft fruit

Summer would not be the same without dishes of soft fruits freshly gathered from the garden, still warm from the sun. You can choose varieties on the basis of fine flavour and, where there is space, for continuity in order to give a succession of early- and late-fruiting plants.

STRAWBERRIES

Short-term crops, strawberry plants last three to four years before they need to be replaced with young plantlets produced on the ends of long runners. For the largest fruits, treat as an annual crop by propagating fresh plants every summer. Save space by growing strawberries as ground cover under other fruits, or as an edging to paths.

Cultivation

Dig and clean the ground thoroughly and work in plenty of decayed manure. Plant in summer, 45–60cm (18–24in) apart each way, in full sun with shelter from cold winds; set plants at their previous level and water well. Mulch before the flower trusses appear. After fruiting, shear or mow the foliage down to 5cm (2in), clear away old straw and feed plants with a general fertilizer.

Other strawberries

Perpetual strawberry varieties fruit in summer and again in autumn; for the best late crops, remove the first flush of blooms, at the same time feeding with general fertilizer. Alpine strawberries are small-fruited, permanent plants that seldom make runners or attract birds – plant 30cm (12in) apart as a decorative edging beside paths or in a herb garden.

RASPBERRIES

Fruits are produced on tall canes that need support, usually with posts and wires arranged as a fence. Plants may also be grown as a small group tied to a central post. Red, yellow and black varieties fruit in summer or autumn.

Cultivation

Dig in plenty of compost or decayed manure, and in autumn or early winter

△ **MULCH STRAWBERRIES** *while still small with straw or with strawberry mats to keep the fruit clean. Pinch off the runners unless they are needed for propagation and net against birds.*

space certified plants 45cm (18in) apart in groups or rows. Shorten any long stems to 23cm (9in) high and, when new growth appears in spring, remove old stems completely: cut them down at ground level. Feed with general fertilizer or mulch with decayed manure every spring. Tie in new canes about 15cm (6in) apart; autumn varieties will fruit the same year, summer varieties the next year. Cut down exhausted autumn-fruiting canes in late winter, just as new stems appear at ground level; cut out old canes of summer varieties after fruiting, making space for new canes to be tied in.

GOOSEBERRIES

One of the easiest soft fruits, and also the first for picking if the young, unripe berries are thinned and used for cooking. There are hundreds of classic green, red, yellow or white varieties, as well as the more recent mildew-resistant or thornless

44

△ **RASPBERRIES DO WELL** *in kitchen gardens and start cropping as strawberries finish.*

△ **STRAWBERRIES** *make ideal container plants and may be brought under glass for forcing.*

◁ PICK WHOLE
BUNCHES *of red
and white currants,
then comb fruits
from the stems
with a dining fork.*

ones: all may be grown as cordons, fans, standards or bushes.

Cultivation

Grow in full sun or light shade, in any well-drained soil. Plant in autumn or early winter, larger plants 1.2m (4ft) and cordons 30cm (12in) apart. Dress with high-potash fertilizer every spring and mulch with compost or decayed manure; water well in dry weather. Start harvesting from late spring onwards, picking alternate fruits and thinning clusters to single berries; the remaining berries can be left to ripen for dessert use. Prune when the crop is finished, cutting out dead or damaged wood and any branches crossing the centre of bushes (for cordons and standards, *see following pages*).

RED AND WHITE CURRANTS

These choice fruits, rarely available in shops, are easily grown on permanently trained plants against walls and fences, where they occupy little space.

Cultivation

Prepare the ground and plant in the same way as for gooseberries. Gather whole strings of currants when fully ripe. Fruit is borne on short, permanent spurs, so prune to create a balanced open framework of branches. Shorten any side shoots to about four or five leaves in summer and still further in winter, to just two buds.

BLACKBERRIES AND OTHER BRAMBLES

❖

Where there is space on a fence or wall, thornless blackberries, loganberries and other hybrid berries are prolific fruits for training on horizontal wires. Cut out all old canes after fruiting each year, replace with the new stems, then mulch well with decayed manure.

BLACKCURRANTS

Compact varieties are available for small gardens, but most kinds make large bushes, a single mature specimen often yielding 5–7kg (11–15lb) of fruit. They are greedy plants that enjoy lavish feeding and a warm position sheltered from frost and cold winds.

Cultivation

Dig and manure the ground well, and in autumn or winter plant two-year-old virus-free bushes, 1.2m (4ft) apart and 5–8cm (2–3in) deeper than they grew before. Cut all stems to 5cm (2in). Each spring-dress with general fertilizer, followed by an 8cm (3in) deep mulch of decayed manure. After two years' growth, prune annually in winter by cutting out one-third of the old, darker branches to make way for vigorous new stems.

TIPS FOR SUCCESS

STRAWBERRIES
❍ Buy stock that is certified virus-free, and propagate only from healthy plants.
❍ Plants may be grown through black plastic sheeting to suppress weeds and reduce the need for watering.
❍ Pick off damaged and mouldy fruits, as diseases spread quickly, especially in a wet summer.
❍ When you need new plants, let the strongest runners root in the ground or peg down the best plantlets in pots.

RASPBERRIES
❍ Bury new plants a little deeper than their previous soil level and firm in.
❍ Water well in dry weather, especially while flowering and fruiting.
❍ Pull up canes that appear more than 20cm (8in) away from rows.
❍ Propagate from healthy suckers growing away from the main plant.

GOOSEBERRIES
❍ Choose plants with a clear single stem or 'leg' to make weeding easier.
❍ Prune bushes to keep centres open for easier picking and to deter mildew.
❍ Do not water when fruits are ripening, as the skins may split.

RED AND WHITE CURRANTS
❍ The same variety can be grown in both full sun and in shade to spread out the crop over many weeks.
❍ Make sure soils are well-drained; mulch light soil to conserve moisture.
❍ Net against birds, as currants are one of their favourite fruits.

BLACKCURRANTS
❍ Reversion virus will usually lead to dwindling yields, so replace every 8–10 years with healthy new plants.
❍ Young stems give the best quality fruit, so feed well to encourage new growth.
❍ Wait until whole bunches are ripe before picking.

45

Growing tree fruits

Where there is room for a specimen tree in the garden, the various types of tree fruit (or 'top fruit') offer produce as well as decorative beauty. Most kinds can also be trained in ornamental forms to create space-saving screens, dividers or garden features, especially if grown on dwarfing rootstocks.

Apples in storage

APPLES

Perhaps the most popular of all tree fruits, this is also the easiest to grow if you choose a regional variety suited to your district and type of soil. Where possible, grow at least two varieties that flower at the same time to ensure good pollination.

Cultivation

Dig and manure the ground well, and make sure it is free-draining. Plant a bare-root tree while dormant, or a container-grown specimen any time the soil is workable. Make a planting hole large enough to take the rootball comfortably, burying it at the same depth as the previous soil mark, and stake or support securely. After planting, and every spring thereafter, spread a 5cm (2in) mulch of decayed manure around the tree or feed with general fertilizer at 70g per sq m (2oz per sq yd). Keep weed-free and water young trees every 10–14 days in dry weather. Young fruitlets naturally thin themselves in early summer, but any clusters remaining should be thinned to one or two fruits. Pick fruits as soon as they part easily from the branch: early varieties should be consumed as soon as they are ripe; later varieties can be stored in a cool, frost-free place, in boxes or perforated polythene bags.

◁ **PRUNED AS A** *mophead standard for a formal lawn feature, this 'James Grieve' dessert apple demonstrates the adaptability of tree fruit.*

PEARS

These need a warmer position than apples but often thrive on poorer soils. As pears flower a few weeks earlier, avoid frosty sites or train trees on a warm wall. Most varieties need a pollination partner nearby in order to set well.

Cultivation

Prepare the ground and plant in the same way as for apples. Trees benefit from a high-nitrogen feed in spring, at a rate of 105g per sq m (3oz per sq yd), followed by a mulch of decayed manure. Thin in early summer, as for apples. Start harvesting as soon as the first varieties turn colour, testing each fruit to see if it comes away easily; most varieties need to be stored for a few weeks to finish ripening (test if they are ready by gently pressing the stalk end).

PLUMS AND GAGES

These succulent fruits are plentiful after a mild spring but are occasionally spoilt by late frosts. The best varieties are sweet and melting, especially gages, which deserve the warmest position, preferably against a warm wall; damsons, on the other hand, are very hardy and may be grown as hedge trees or windbreaks.

Cultivation

Grow in full sun with protection from frosts. Prepare, plant and cultivate in the same way as for apples, and feed with nitrogen every spring (*see Pears, above*). Thin fruits after the natural midsummer drop, and support laden branches that might break. Harvest fruits when they part easily with their stalks, especially before heavy rain, which can cause ripening fruits to split; use immediately, freezing or bottling any surplus.

CHERRIES

Dessert (sweet) varieties are very choice, but you will need to protect them from birds; culinary (acid) varieties are less popular with birds and are easier to grow in shady gardens. The two types are pruned in different ways. Choose a dwarfing rootstock and a self-fertile variety if you are growing a single tree.

Cultivation

Prepare, plant and cultivate in the same way as for apples (above). Add plenty of compost or manure to light soils, and choose a sunny position for sweet cherries; full sun or light shade for acid kinds. Fruits do not need thinning.

PEACHES, NECTARINES AND APRICOTS

❖

These flower very early and succeed only where springs are frost-free and summers warm and sunny. Try growing one in the greenhouse, or against a warm wall where it can be covered with a curtain of polythene sheeting against frost and also peach leaf curl disease. Fruits need rigorous thinning to 15cm (6in) apart for good size (as shown); varieties are self-fertile but may need hand-pollination in a cold season.

Harvest as soon as they are ripe and before they split, picking or cutting complete with stalks. Use immediately and freeze or bottle the surplus.

◁ MOST PEAR
varieties enjoy heat and summer sun and training a pear tree as a fan against a warm wall will ensure good crops in a cool garden.

TIPS FOR SUCCESS

APPLES
○ Avoid diseases by choosing resistant varieties rather than treating problems when they arise.
○ Prop up heavily laden branches to prevent breakage.
○ Grow grass right up to the stem of vigorous, established trees to control their growth.
○ Growing single cordons enables you to build up a collection of apple varieties in a small space.

PEARS
○ Gather up young fruitlets that fall early, as these often contain pests.
○ Good drainage is very important, although pears are also less drought-tolerant than apples.
○ Pears do not ripen all together: trees will need picking over several times.
○ Pears need less pruning than apples and tolerate harder pruning back.

PLUMS AND GAGES
○ Even self-fertile varieties crop more heavily with a compatible pollinator that blooms at the same time.
○ Only prune when trees are actively growing, as wounds then heal quickly.
○ Train as fans, not cordons or espaliers.
○ 'Pixie' is a dwarf rootstock to consider.

CHERRY
○ Prune during active growth to avoid disease problems.
○ Water copiously and regularly in a dry season, especially wall-trained trees.

POLLINATION
○ If you can grow only one variety of a tree fruit, choose a self-fertile kind.
○ Most varieties (including self-fertile ones) crop better with a pollinating partner, another variety that flowers at the same time and, in the case of plums and cherries, which belongs to a compatible group. Consult an informative catalogue before buying.

47

Pruning and training fruit

Most soft and tree fruits will give a crop of some kind if left to develop unchecked from one season to the next. However, pruning and training are valuable methods of controlling growth. They help to create plants that are healthier, more attractive and, above all, consistently give heavy yields of high-quality produce.

DEFINITIONS

Pruning involves the removal of all surplus or misplaced growth, partly to maintain size but also to stimulate later development in a particular way – changing direction, for example, or encouraging fruit rather than leaf buds.

Training is the complementary art of steering this growth in ways that suit the type of plant and its position, with the aim of improving both its appearance and its yield. While the same basic principles are involved in creating all trained forms (see panel), in practice the ultimate shape you want will determine how they are applied.

BUSHES

This is an easy and productive shape to form and maintain, although it can occupy a lot of space in a small garden. Standards and half-standards are simply bushes on single, straight stems of varying heights. A young bush should have three to five main branches, which will develop if the main stem of a one-year-old tree is pruned back after planting. Shorten these branches by half in winter to produce secondary branches. The following winter, select the best seven or eight shoots as the permanent branches, and shorten them by half again. Thereafter, tip these main

△ **CORDON-TRAINED PEARS** *make efficient use of a wall or fence and allow different varieties to be grown for cross-pollination.*

branches each winter, and shorten side shoots to three to five buds to maintain shape.

CORDONS

A cordon is a single-stemmed apple, pear, gooseberry or redcurrant, grown upright or at an oblique angle of about 45°; multiple cordons have two or more parallel stems, each formed and pruned in the same way. Tie the leader (main stem) to a strong cane or stake, leaving

48

△ **ACID CHERRY VARIETIES**, *such as 'Morello', are ideal candidates for fan-training on a wall.*

ROOTSTOCKS

Most tree fruit varieties are grafted on to rootstocks of known vigour, so the eventual tree's size is predictable: this can reduce the amount of pruning needed to maintain trained form, and helps trees adjust to different soil conditions. Each fruit has its own types of rootstock, which can range from very vigorous to very dwarfing. Names and types vary between countries: check in a good catalogue to ensure that you are choosing the right kind for your region and site.

△ **ESPALIERS ARE** *space-saving forms that allow top fruits such as apples to be trained productively in narrow beds or beside paths.*

PRUNING TIPS

❖

Keep bushes goblet-shaped, with open centres formed by removing any branches that grow inwards.

On wall-trained fruit, cut out any misplaced shoots growing towards or away from the wall before they are too big.

Do not try to grow tip-bearing apple varieties as cordons, fans or espaliers.

Always use sharp tools, think carefully before pruning any stem, and cut to a bud facing in the direction you want its shoot to grow.

Train fruit securely on strong stakes (and on wires where appropriate); check ties regularly to make sure they are not too tight.

it unpruned until it reaches full height; then prune the same way as new side shoots. Shorten these in midsummer to four or five leaves, and prune further the following winter to one or two buds.

ESPALIERS

These are trained trees, with single upright main stems and pairs of straight branches (arms) arranged in tiers 38–45cm (15–18in) apart and running in opposite directions on horizontal wires. Most espaliers have two, three or four pairs of arms, but the low-growing form called a 'stepover' tree has one pair about 38cm (15in) above ground.

Start training an espalier by planting a one-year-old maiden and cutting its stem just below the bottom wire. From the several shoots then produced, train the topmost one vertically, and the next two to each side at an angle of 45°. The following winter, lower these two side branches to the bottom wire and tie them securely; cut the main stem just below the next wire. Repeat each year until the top wire is reached. Each side arm is then trained and pruned like a cordon (*see above*).

FANS

The fan is a decorative form ideal for many fruits, but most often used for plums, peaches and cherries. Start training in the same way as for an espalier, but leave the first two side branches tied in at an angle, shortening

SUMMER AND WINTER PRUNING

❖

Pruning in mid- and late summer benefits all fruits trained in restricted forms – such as cordons, fans and espaliers – by redirecting their growth into developing fruiting spurs and buds, and so increasing overall yields. Winter pruning applies to all fruit, and is used to remove dead and diseased stems, limit size and control shape. To avoid exposing wounds to disease, stone fruits such as plums, cherries and peaches are winter-pruned in early spring, when the buds first start to burst.

49

them in late winter to about 45cm (18in) long. During the summer, tie in the strongest four or five shoots that form on each arm, spreading them out evenly like the ribs of a fan. Late the following winter, shorten these by one-third to produce further side branches for tying in to create the main framework.

Fruiting side shoots are produced on these branches and pruned according to the type of fruit. Treat apples, pears and sweet cherries in the same way, by forming permanent spurs (*see cordons above*). With plum, peach and acid cherry, cut out the side shoots after fruiting to make way for new shoots.

Planning a herb garden

Whether you grow just a few basic herbs or collect all possible varieties, culinary herbs are essential kitchen-garden accessories. Each contributes unique fragrance and beauty to its surroundings, and will add supreme flavour to dishes and salads when they are gathered fresh from the garden.

CHOOSING A SITE

For best results, choose a position in full sun with shelter from cold, drying winds. Easy access is important: a site near the kitchen door would be ideal for a small herb collection. A larger, well-stocked herb garden can be an ornamental feature, with shaped beds of plants, paths and perhaps a seat. A bed 1.2m by 1.8m (4ft by 6ft) will easily accommodate basic *bouquet garni* herbs (parsley, thyme, sage, marjoram and bay), with mint, chives and tarragon: arrange with the taller plants in the centre or at the back. Where space is limited, grow your herbs in containers on a sunny patio or balcony.

Larger herb gardens need to be planned on paper, so draw a scale plan first. Decide on the shape, remembering that simplicity is a virtue, and include paths for access. Square or circular beds provide a disciplined outline for the varied plant shapes, although a relaxed cottage garden arrangement can be pleasing. Choose the herbs you know and use, adding others if there is space.

PREPARATION AND CARE

Mark out your plan on the ground. Dig over the site, working in plenty of garden compost or bought bagged compost; add gravel or grit to heavy soils for improved drainage. Fork out all perennial weeds, as these are hard to remove after planting. Beds can be edged with boards, bricks

◁ **IN THIS POTAGER STYLE** *herb garden, a pot of lemon balm forms the centrepiece to geometric beds planted with silver thyme, purple sage, marjoram, tarragon and bay.*

or tiles, and paths finished with bark, gravel or a suitable hard surface.

Sow or plant new herbs in spring, although container-grown plants can be introduced at any time. Place perennial herbs first, as these provide a permanent framework, then position annuals and biennials among them, aiming for a satisfying balance of shapes and sizes. Site special herbs prominently – silver or grey plants where they catch the sun, aromatic sage or rosemary where it will be brushed in passing. Water in after planting, and on light soils mulch with compost or bark (on heavy ground use gravel or grit to aid drainage).

Leafy herbs need regular watering, whereas woody perennials and seed-bearing plants require very little. Trim perennials annually after flowering, and cut back herbs such as mint in summer to stimulate further young foliage. Cut down and clear away all dead growth in late autumn.

RESTRAINING INVASIVE HERBS

Herbs such as tarragon and most mints spread vigorously by underground runners and will threaten neighbouring plants unless restrained. Surround with a barrier of slates buried vertically in the ground, or plant in a bottomless bucket buried to its rim. A large plastic bag with a perforated base, filled with soil and buried just out of sight, is a good substitute.

◁ CHOOSE A SUNNY SITE *for a herb garden. This new one, backed by a protective wall, has square, timber-edged beds with paths of bark chippings.*

SPECIAL USES

Herbs can be used as design elements around the garden. Sweet bay may be trained as topiary or as an ornamental tree, while closely planted rosemary makes a classic hedge. Use mat-forming herbs such as marjoram, thyme and pennyroyal for edging or plant in paving joints to make an aromatic path.

▽ MANY HERBS *are naturally prostrate or bushy and eventually sprawl informally over the edges of beds. Here, bright green parsley softens the angularity of paving slabs.*

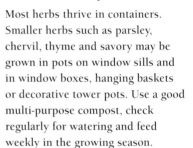

HERBS IN CONTAINERS
❖

Most herbs thrive in containers. Smaller herbs such as parsley, chervil, thyme and savory may be grown in pots on window sills and in window boxes, hanging baskets or decorative tower pots. Use a good multi-purpose compost, check regularly for watering and feed weekly in the growing season.

HARVESTING HERBS

Harvesting herbs regularly helps to keep plants neat and shapely, so gather leaves and shoots as required. For drying, freezing and other forms of preservation, pick them on a dry morning during or just before flowering, when their flavour is most intense. Spread out or hang up stems to dry in warm shade, or freeze the leaves immediately.

51

Basic culinary herbs

Cookery enthusiasts consider five classic herbs essential for flavouring many dishes: bay, marjoram, parsley, sage and thyme; they are often combined together as a bouquet garni. They are all easy to grow and will form the nucleus of any herb collection.

▽ **PURPLE-LEAVED SAGE**, *tall angelica and feathery bronze fennel are combined with other decorative plants like alchemilla, alliums, iris and French lavender.*

BAY (*Laurus nobilis*)
An evergreen Mediterranean tree growing up to 6m (20ft) high, with tough, glossy leaves. It is usually grown as a bushy shrub or clipped into simple topiary shapes such as mophead standards. Slightly susceptible to frost, especially while young, bay can be grown in a container and brought under cover in winter.

Grow in well-drained soil or soil-based potting compost, in full sun with shelter from cold winds. Feeding is unnecessary, but plants benefit from occasional watering in dry weather. Trim to shape in early summer and again in autumn for formal topiary. Propagate by cuttings of side shoots, taken with a heel of old wood.

Harvest leaves at any time for immediate use or drying in darkness.

MARJORAM (*Origanum*)
Highly decorative shrubby herbs up to 60cm (2ft) high, reasonably hardy if grown in full sun and well-drained soil. Pot marjoram (*O. onites*) is very hardy, with a milder flavour than sweet marjoram (*O. marjorana*); oregano or wild marjoram (*O. vulgare*) is very pungent and available in many ornamental forms.

Grow in dry, warm soil, with a little lime if known to be acid. Trim hard in late autumn, and lift one or two plants for use indoors in winter. Propagate by sowing in early spring under glass, by division in spring or autumn, or from cuttings in summer.

Harvest fresh at any time, or gather shoots just before flowering for drying slowly in darkness.

△ **A WINDOW BOX** *makes an excellent miniature herb garden, offering convenient pickings of rosemary, sage and thyme.*

△ **BAY TREES** *are traditionally grown in terracotta pots, where young plants can be clipped and shaped to use as formal ornaments.*

Marjoram (Origanum vulgare 'Gold Tip')

Parsley (Petroselinum crispum)

Thymes, including golden and variegated forms

PARSLEY (*Petroselinum crispum*)

A leafy biennial, usually grown as an annual, the common curly kinds make dense, decorative plants 30cm (12in) tall; the flat-leafed French or Italian kind has a stronger flavour and can reach 60cm (2ft) high.

Grow from seed, sown thinly outdoors in rich, moist soil, in late spring and again in late summer for succession over winter; seedlings are often slow to appear. Thin to 15–23cm (6–9in) apart, and keep well-watered at all times. Earlier crops may be started under glass in pots. Transplant a few late-summer seedlings to pots or a greenhouse border for winter use. Harvest sprigs as needed, and cut whole plants before they flower for freezing in bags or in ice cubes.

SAGE (*Salvia officinalis*)

Large, handsome bushes with subtle leaf colours, as much at home in a flower border as in the herb garden. Plants are easily grown but resent wet conditions in winter, so work plenty of grit into heavy soils before planting. Pineapple sage (*S. rutilans*) is tender and best grown under glass, where its scarlet flowers appear in winter.

Grow in fertile, well-drained soil, in full sun with shelter from cold winds. Clip annually to shape after flowering, and renew plants after four to five years before their stems become bare. Propagate plain green forms from seeds sown outdoors in spring, all kinds from 8cm (3in) summer cuttings of side shoots pulled off with a heel.

Harvest leaves and shoot tips at any time, or just before flowering for drying in warm shade.

THYME (*Thymus*)

There are many different thymes for various purposes: the upright common thyme (*T. vulgaris*) is perhaps best for culinary use, while the many forms of creeping wild thyme (*T. serpyllum*) are neat, mat-forming plants for edging or growing in between paving slabs, and also for collecting in thyme pots and other containers.

Grow in full sun, in dry, well-drained soil with low fertility; add plenty of grit to heavier soils for good drainage. Trim several times in spring and summer, especially straight after flowering, to keep plants dense and neat, and replace after four or five

years. Propagate by seed or division in spring, by cuttings from side shoots in summer, or by layering in autumn.

Harvest the leaves and tips of shoots as needed to use fresh, or just as the flowers open for drying.

CULTIVATION TIPS

53

- In cold areas, the willow-leaved bay (*L. nobilis* f. *angustifolia*) often proves a little hardier than the common form.

- Marjoram makes an ideal plant for edges, joints in paving and for hanging baskets.

- Seeds of parsley often fail because of drought; hasten germination by soaking seeds in warm water overnight, and keep the soil consistently moist until seedlings appear.

- Red-, purple- and gold-variegated forms of sage make attractive pot plants, but are less hardy than the plain green kinds.

- Plant upright varieties of thyme 10–15cm (4–6in) apart and clip regularly to make a dwarf hedge around a small herb bed.

Making a herb collection

A larger herb bed might include any of these popular, easily grown culinary herbs, each with an individual flavour and indispensable in its own way. Explore the subtle, aromatic differences between varieties, perhaps growing them first in pots until they become more familiar.

△ **BASIL COMES IN** *several varieties, offering good looks as well as distinct flavours. In addition to sweet basil and bush basil, are the less common holy basil, cinnamon basil and 'Green Ruffles'.*

54

BASIL (*Ocimum basilicum*)
A tender, annual herb, available in a huge range of varied colours, forms and fragrances, and familiar as an essential ingredient of much Mediterranean cooking, especially as a complement to tomatoes. In cold gardens, plants are best grown in pots indoors or in a sheltered place outside.

Grow from seed sown in warmth in early spring, and again in midsummer for succession. Pot up seedlings individually in soil-based compost and either pot on for container culture or plant out after hardening off, 15cm (6in) apart, in a sheltered, sunny place. Water whenever dry, and pinch out growing tips regularly to encourage bushy growth and delay flowering.

Harvest leaves as needed; just before flowering or the first frosts, cut plants down and dry very slowly in darkness.

CHIVES (*Allium schoenoprasum*)
Hardy, perennial bulbs forming neat clumps of grassy foliage with a pleasant, onion-like flavour; the mauve flowers are pretty as an edible garnish. Use as edging plants and keep some in pots for use out of season.

Grow from seeds sown in spring, outdoors in rows or in modules under glass, or buy plants in late spring. Space small groups 23cm (9in) apart, in moist, fertile soil in full sun or light shade. Water regularly in dry weather. Cut back once or twice to prompt plenty of young, new growth. Propagate by division in autumn, renewing large clumps every few years and replanting in fresh soil.

Harvest leaves and flowers as needed; larger quantities just before flowering for freezing.

MINT (*Mentha*)
There are many different forms of mint, all with wonderful flavours, but they tend to invade the surrounding ground

▽ **THE VARIOUS MINTS,** *with their invasive roots, are best confined in pots, while chives in bloom make very colourful container plants.*

◁ ROSEMARY *can mature into a large shrub when grown, as here, in a well-drained, raised bed against a warm wall.*

EDGES AND HEDGES

When planning the garden layout, remember that herbs are ready-made designer plants. Prostrate varieties such as Corsican mint, penny-royal and many thymes or marjorams form mats of pretty foliage to spill over edges and fill gaps in paving. Rosemary, lavender and hyssop are all bushy perennials that withstand clipping to make neat dwarf hedges for framing or dividing beds.

unless restrained. The best for mint sauce is apple mint (*M. suaveolens*) or Bowles' mint (*M.* x *villosa alopecuroides*).

Grow mint in moist, deeply dug and manured soil, in a bottomless bucket or plastic bag with a few drainage holes, buried to the rim in the ground. A lightly shaded position is best for summer supplies; keep well-watered in dry weather. Cut back some stems at midsummer for a late supply of young growth. Roots may be boxed up in autumn for forcing under glass. Propagate by root division, every three or four years for established clumps.

Harvest leaves and shoot tips as needed, just before flowering for freezing or making mint jelly.

ROSEMARY (*Rosmarinus officinalis*)
These fairly hardy evergreens, varying from tall upright shrubs to charmingly prostrate varieties, all have dense, pointed leaves and blue, white or pink flowers in spring. They are ornamental as well as aromatic plants, attractive to bees when flowering.

Grow rosemary in well-drained soil, in full sun with shelter from cold winds. Plant in spring and protect young plants with fleece in winter. Plants may also be grown in pots, especially the less hardy, variegated kinds. Clip to shape after flowering. Propagate from cuttings of side shoots in summer, or by layering in autumn.

Harvest sprigs for use as needed; do this at flowering time for drying slowly in shade.

TARRAGON (*Artemisia dracunculus*)
French tarragon is considered to be the best-flavoured but is not always reliably hardy in cold gardens, whereas the more robust Russian tarragon (*A. d. dracunculoides*) is a coarser plant in both form and flavour.

Grow tarragon in well-drained soil, in a sunny dry position with shelter from cold winds, and confine the invasive plants in the same way as for mint. Growing a few plants in a cold frame will extend the season. Cut plants

EXTENDING YOUR CHOICE

Growing herbs is compulsive, and you can often find room for another variety. These culinary species make useful additions to any collection and many are decorative enough to be grown in the flower garden.

ANGELICA (*Angelica archangelica*)
Tall, stately biennial for moist places.

BERGAMOT (*Monarda didyma*)
Cottage-garden plant with bright flowers beloved by bees.

BORAGE (*Borago officinalis*)
Blue-flowered annual for summer drinks and salads.

CHERVIL (*Anthriscus cerefolium*)
Lacy annual with a sweet, aromatic flavour.

DILL (*Anethum graveolens*)
Pungent annual grown for its leaves or seeds.

FENNEL (*Foeniculum vulgare*)
Tall foliage plant with aniseed-flavoured seeds.

LEMON BALM (*Melissa officinalis*)
Vigorous, ground-covering perennial with sweet, lemony flavour.

SAVORY (*Satureja* species)
Aromatic summer annual and winter perennials.

55

down after the first frosts and protect the roots with a mulch of straw or autumn leaves. Propagate by root division of mature plants every three or four years.

Harvest the leafy shoots of this distinctively aromatic plant as required, or at the start of flowering for freezing or drying slowly in warmth.

Productive ideas for small gardens

Getting value for space becomes an urgent priority in a tiny garden. The limitations of a balcony, rooftop, terrace plot or basement area might seem disheartening, but with a little ingenuity you can devise ways to turn every nook and cranny to productive use.

◁ **A DISCARDED** *saucepan provides a cool, deep root run for hungry crops such as strawberries.*

ASSESSING THE SPACE

It is rare for anyone to find they have room to grow everything, and the amount of ground most gardeners have at their disposal tempers ambition and challenges preconceptions. Classic kitchen gardening practices assumed huge areas of land, and growing methods evolved that are difficult to scale down to modern proportions. But most plants will grow wherever there is a pocket of soil, and even the least hospitable place can be made to bloom and to fruit.

As suggested earlier, make a shortlist of indispensable crops and special favourites. Explore miniature or dwarf varieties of these (see page 40 for vegetables), and find out their individual needs and preferences: there are few that will not grow in containers and other restricted places, and early varieties of most crops take up the least space.

Appraise less obvious sites such as a shed roof, the top of a wall or the side of a flight of steps for a row of pots. Walls, fences and even hedges can be exploited for trained fruit, dwarf trees and climbing vegetables; aerial containers can be suspended from hooks, wires or eaves. You could frame a gateway with cordon fruits, turn an alleyway into a productive tunnel, create a bamboo-cane porch of runner beans, and embellish steps and drain covers with tubs and troughs of herbs and salads. All it takes is the motivation.

◁ **BOXES OF** *treated wood make adaptable containers that blend with other natural materials and insulate roots from light frost.*

SALAD BOWLS

Most plants grow naturally as part of a community, a preference that can be turned to good use when growing crops in containers. Instead of single pots, choose stone or metal troughs, wide, shallow bowls, recycled wooden boxes or large bins. Spread a generous layer of composted manure in the bottom, fill with a rich soil-based compost such as John Innes No 3, and then plant them with a collection of complementary crops. Most salads grow well with each other; a central bamboo wigwam for cucumbers would also support peas on twiggy sticks arranged around the base; or beans could be planted to twine up sweet corn through a ground cover of summer squashes. Complete the composition with trailers such as New Zealand spinach or wild strawberries planted around the edges.

HANGING GARDENS

Traditional hanging baskets can house many crops, from parsley to trailing tomatoes, but they sometimes demand copious and frequent watering. Plant sleeves or pouches are a more easily maintained alternative. These are made from long sections of plastic tubing, perforated with a number of planting pockets. They are filled with compost, planted up with seedlings or plug plants, and suspended vertically from a bracket or horizontally from window

◁ **MAKE USE** *of all vertical surfaces for suspending containers of small food plants and summer flowers.*

WINDOW GARDENS

Window sills, inside and out, can be turned to profitable use. An indoor sill is ideal for raising plants from seed, for sprouting mung beans, alfalfa and other nutritious seed crops, and also for growing on seedlings if you turn them every day or so to prevent their leaning to the light. Cut-and-come-again seedling crops in trays can be kept here for their whole productive life.

An outdoor window box may be used all year round if it is deep enough and filled with rich compost. Or use composted bark to turn the box into a plunge bed for pots of vegetables started elsewhere and moved out as they approach maturity, before being exchanged for others. Make sure the box is firmly supported, for it will be very heavy when full. If it is exposed to strong winds, arrange screens of sacking or fleece at the sides as windbreaks, and use jam jars or miniature cloches to protect plants in cold weather.

EXPLOITING HARD AREAS

Although essential for access in larger gardens, a path may be a luxury where space is rationed; disperse stepping stones among plants instead, or make a pavement of broken slabs and prostrate herbs. Where the whole garden is hard

surface, however, other growing areas must be found. You might be able to lift some slabs or stones to create planting pockets, or build raised beds with brick surrounds; a second skin of brickwork along a wall will produce a useful planting area if the cavity is filled with drainage rubble and then compost.

Tower pots or pocket planters are designed for strawberries but are equally good for herbs, lettuces, dwarf beans or bush tomatoes; they take up little ground space. Growing bags, laid flat on the ground or cut in half and stood on end, make improvised vegetable beds and can be enclosed in a timber box to hide their sometimes garish colours. You can use two bags, one on top of the other, and cut or pierce holes in the plastic so that plants can root through to the bottom – this will then sustain greedy crops such as runner beans, cucumbers and squashes, which can be trained on strings suspended from the eaves or a window sill.

sills. Although intended for summer bedding, they produce lush crops of herbs, salads and leaf crops, and even strawberries.

MIXED ABILITY CROPS

The bewildering range of vegetable varieties now available can work to your advantage, because you will usually have the choice of early or late, dwarf or tall, fast growing or maincrop kinds. Instead of growing a row or block of each type to spread the harvest, try mixing early, mid-season and late varieties in a single sowing so that a small area or single container can be productive over a longer period. Some seedsmen now sell blends of this kind. Combining tall and dwarf varieties is also successful – tall peas, which are prolific but do not crop near their base, can be mixed with a dwarf variety that flowers while still small, for example.

57

A SELF-SERVICE HERB TABLE

❖

A deep wooden box supported on four sturdy legs makes an excellent raised garden for smaller herbs such as thyme, marjoram, basil, parsley and chives. Treat the timber with preservative or line it with plastic and then spread a layer of drainage crocks or stones in the bottom. Fill with soil-based compost, arrange the herbs in position and finish the surface with a mulch of gravel. If you entertain outdoors, position one or two pieces of slate where guests can rest their plates while helping themselves to a pinch of herbs.

Dealing with pests and diseases

Every garden supports a cosmopolitan community of organisms, some of them dependable allies, but others a potential threat to our plants' welfare. It is important to distinguish between them in your efforts to grow healthy food crops, and to choose an effective but unobtrusive policy of pest and disease control.

A HOLISTIC APPROACH

Escaping garden pests and diseases is impossible. As an important part of natural life cycles and processes, they will arrive sooner or later and inevitably cause you some concern. How serious you consider their incidence to be, however, depends on your growing methods and also on your attitude to plant disorders.

If you maintain a fertile soil and a balanced mixture of vigorous, well-tended plants, ailments will rarely be disastrous. By taking basic precautions to reduce risks, practising sensible garden hygiene and encouraging natural sources of control such as predators, it is usually possible to establish an acceptable, low and stable level of pests and diseases that only occasionally threaten to grow out of hand. When this does happen, it is often the result of mismanagement – lack of watering or over-zealous use of chemicals.

COMMON PESTS

The population of insects in a garden is huge and diverse. Just a fraction of them is hostile, and then usually on a seasonal, often predictable basis. The commonest outdoor pests are slugs and snails, aphids, caterpillars and, in a dry season, red spider mites; vine weevils and scale insects are minor but locally increasing problems. Other pests such as brassica whitefly or woodlice are an irritation rather than a threat.

The reasons why some pests are common are often environmental. Slugs and snails, for example, thrive in moist conditions and multiply quickly in a wet season or where the ground is watered regularly; they have catholic tastes and can usually find something to eat. A milder climate encourages a population of butterflies and moths, welcome in some quarters but not when their caterpillars feast on garden plants. Most such pests, however, respond to simple treatment.

Fly paper

Control methods

• Physical barriers are useful. Fleece retains warmth and protects susceptible crops such as cabbages and carrots against egg-laying female insects. Netting keeps birds away from brassicas and ripening fruit, and cats off seedbeds.
• A circle of crushed eggshells, lime or fresh soot round individual plants sometimes deters slugs and snails, although these are easily caught by hand after rain or on a damp night.
• Manual control often helps – you can remove caterpillars, wipe off aphids and pick out large soil pests when digging.
• Traps are effective against slugs and insect fruit pests, while biological methods of introducing predators and parasites can treat a number of others.
• Finally, clear away favourite hiding places and alternative hosts, maintain strong plants and vigorous growth, and use resistant varieties where possible. Chemical treatment should then be needed only as a last resort.

58

GARDENER'S ALLIES
❖

Learn to distinguish your friends from your foes. Slow, black millipedes, for example, are vegetarian and feed on plants, whereas fast-moving centipedes and many beetles are hunters that prey on insect pests. Encourage existing predators, such as the birds in your garden: thrushes control snails, while blue-tits eat enormous numbers of aphids. The larvae of ladybirds, lacewings and hoverflies are common aphid predators – encourage the adults by planting flat-topped nectar-rich flowers such as sedums and achillea for them to browse on. A small pond will attract toads and frogs, which are greedy insectivores.

Blue-tit

COMMON DISEASES

Plant diseases are often more sinister than pests, because they seem harder to control and threaten to escalate if not treated. They are mostly caused by fungal, bacterial or viral pathogens that spread from already infected plants. Some are undoubtedly serious but they commonly strike only where plants are stressed or ailing, and (as with pests) promoting vigorous and positive plant health is a sound policy.

The commonest diseases include mildews and moulds, black spot, rusts and rots, virus diseases, and more specialised organisms such as peach leaf curl, potato scab or tomato blight. It is worth noting that plants are not immortal, and an outbreak of disease will often indicate the victim is past its best and should be pulled up. This is a

△ THE TOP HALF *of a clear plastic bottle makes a good cloche to protect individual transplants; remove its cap for ventilation in mild weather.*

△ SUSPEND PHEROMONE TRAPS *from fruit tree branches to lure male insect pests to their doom and so reduce the numbers of fertile eggs.*

commendable old-fashioned approach with many vegetables, which are seldom worth treating once infected, but should be removed to prevent the disease from spreading.

Control methods

• Avoidance is the best control measure. Only plant healthy stock that looks in good condition and, in the case of fruit and potatoes, is certified disease-free.

• Choose resistant seed varieties where possible, rotate crops (see page 14) to reduce risks, and disperse plants among unrelated neighbours – remember that many weeds are regular alternative disease hosts.

• On difficult sites, choose appropriate varieties: certain apple cultivars, for example, develop canker on wet soils.

• Try to avoid cultural oversights that invite trouble. Waterlogged potting compost breeds damping off disease; mildew thrives with poor ventilation; mistimed pruning can cause silver leaf disease or scab.

• Wash greenhouses regularly and clean dirty pots, trays and labels with

disinfectant. Only use fresh potting compost, and keep open bags sealed against possible infection.

• Learn to recognize warning signs such as a yellowing leaf or distorted shoot. These may be early symptoms which will not develop any further if the affected leaf or shoot is picked or pruned off promptly.

• Isolate infected container plants, burn diseased material and control high numbers of aphids, which spread a variety of diseases.

• Keep a systemic fungicide in reserve for serious outbreaks – it may halt a fungal infection, but rarely affects bacterial diseases.

• Never panic. Often an apparent disease symptom is merely a physiological disorder that will go away when the weather improves or the affected plant is fed with the missing trace elements.

59

Weeds and weeding

Nature abhors a vacuum, nowhere more so than in disturbed soil which seems to contain an inexhaustible reservoir of weed seeds, just waiting for the cue to germinate. They compete efficiently with cultivated plants for space and nutrients, and should be firmly subdued by one or more of the methods outlined here.

MAKING THE DISTINCTION

As gardeners we all have an acquaintance with weeds, but we might differ in our perception of what actually constitutes one. The difference between weeds and wildflowers, for example, is debatable. The generally accepted definition of a weed is any unwelcome plant, or a plant in the wrong place, although the essayist Emerson more wisely described it as 'a plant whose virtues have not yet been discovered'.

In a closely packed kitchen garden, especially if it is small, there will be no spare room for weeds, which can become a serious problem if allowed to establish themselves. They invade and dominate crops in their search for water, light and plant nutrients and, perhaps more ominously, subvert attempts to avoid pests and diseases by acting as alternative hosts for many of these. It is unrealistic to expect to eradicate weeds totally, but fortunately keeping them down to acceptable levels is not difficult.

Bindweed

DISCOURAGING WEEDS

It is variously said that one year's seeding means seven (or ten, or more) years' weeding, and there is truth in these gloomy warnings. Weeds are notorious colonizers, able to multiply and survive with the least encouragement, and their great tenacity is partly due to their vigorous seed production and dispersal mechanisms. Pulling up weeds before they flower is a top priority, and you should never leave them lying around because many continue ripening their seeds even when out of the ground.

Red clover

Regular cultivation by hoeing or forking the surface will discourage annuals and exhaust some perennials. If you dig the plot or prepare a seedbed, leave the soil to settle for a week or so – many weed seeds near the surface will germinate after a few days and can be lightly hoed off to leave a cleaner bed. Plant crops close together to shade the soil and suppress weed growth, and try watering individual plants in dry weather instead of soaking a whole area, which can trigger germination.

CONTROL METHODS

Thorough soil preparation at the start of the season is the first step, followed by a regular routine of hoeing, hand-pulling and mulching between early spring and early or mid-autumn. These basic physical methods are normally sufficient, even with the more challenging problem of deep-rooted perennials – your persistence will eventually triumph over theirs. With the exception of derelict sites and perhaps whole-season weed control on paths, there should be little need for chemical herbicides, which are in any case difficult to apply precisely in a closely planted small garden. If you do resort to a weedkiller, choose a day when there is little wind to cause spray drift, apply with a watering can fitted with a trickle bar, and either reserve the can for this purpose or wash it out thoroughly after use.

ANNUAL WEEDS

Although they are prolific self-seeders, annuals have shallow roots and are the easiest weeds to tackle. Hoeing in dry, sunny weather usually kills them outright, and brings more seeds to the surface for later cultivation so that their numbers gradually decline. An effective alternative is mulching, which denies the seeds light and suppresses germination – since it also reduces the amount of deep cultivation needed, other dormant seeds are left undisturbed well

Creeping buttercup

60

below the surface. Provided they are not flowering, annuals can be safely composted or dug in to return nutrients to the soil.

PERENNIALS

Perennial weeds are very efficient subsoilers, opening up the ground and retrieving minerals from deep down, but they can cause much more mischief than annuals. They seed themselves in the same way, but also multiply by other, vegetative methods – deep underground runners and horizontal roots, surface layers, and even bulbils in the case of oxalis. Any fragment left in the soil can regenerate, often more vigorously: cutting a single root of couch grass, for example, awakens several dormant buds to start rooting simultaneously. For this reason it is crucial to search out as much of the roots as possible during digging, and to stay alert for any regrowth, which can be hoed or pulled up.

△ WOVEN PLASTIC *sheeting is a tough and durable weed-suppressant mulch that admits water to the soil while delaying its evaporation.*

WEED DISPOSAL

As with any other plant, weeds absorb nutrients from the soil and then release them again as they decay, so put them to good use. They are an important waste ingredient of compost heaps, but avoid using diseased or seeding annuals and the roots of perennials unless you can guarantee sufficient heat in the heap to destroy them – live nettle, ground elder and couch roots are robust enough to run riot, even when buried deep in a compost heap. In summer you can spread them in the sun until completely dry, then compost them for their particularly rich mineral content. Alternatively, burn them and spread the ashes on the heap as a source of potash.

◁ HOEING IS *a gentle exercise and, if done regularly while weeds are small, can prevent them menacing young seedlings.*

CLEARING FRESH GROUND

Cleaning up a neglected plot is a serious undertaking. The weeds will be well established, many of them with deep, tough roots, and physically removing them is not light work, so you should divide the task into easy stages.

○ Cutting down topgrowth is the first priority: you can use shears, a sickle or strimmer, or a mower with an oscillating cutter-bar for most weeds. Chop down hard woody stems with secateurs or loppers.

○ Once this material is removed for composting or burning, you can reduce topgrowth further by running a rotary mower over the plot (check first for hidden obstacles, though). Then decide if you need to clear the whole area in one go; if not, part can be kept under control with the mower while you cultivate one section at a time.

○ Wholesale slaughter with a weedkiller is one popular option, using a systemic herbicide such as glyphosate applied when new active growth is visible.

○ Organic gardeners prefer to smother weeds by spreading old carpets and cardboard on the ground to deny them light and air, but it can take a whole year before determined weeds are dead.

○ An effective alternative is to chop or skim off the top 5cm (2in) of soil and weeds with a spade, and then dig the exposed soil which will break up much more easily. Cut the removed layer into turves as you go, stack these and cover with black polythene for a year to kill the weeds, then return the soil to the garden.

61

Bold page numbers indicate illustrations

A

angelica **52**, 55
apples 46, **46**, 47
  in containers 42
  fan-training 49
  pruning and training 9, 48-9, **49**
  'step-over' 9, 49
apricots 47
artichokes see globe artichokes;
  Jerusalem artichokes
asparagus 7, 9, 15, 35
aspect 6
aubergines 39, **39**

B

basil 42, 54, **54**
bay 50, **50**, 51, 52, **52**, 53
beans 24-5, **24-5**
  in containers 56
  crop rotation 15
  on fences and walls 9
  growing in borders 9
  seeds 11
bedding plants 9
beds, raised **13**, 57
beetroot 26, **26**, 27
  growing in borders 9, 30
  growing times 14
  mini-vegetables 41
bergamot 55
blackberries 9, 45, **45**
blackcurrants 19, 45
blueberries 42
borage **8**, 55
borders, growing vegetables in 9
broad beans 9, 14, 24, 25
broccoli 29
  growing times 14
  siting 15
Brussels sprouts 28, **28**, 29
  growing in borders 9
  growing times 14
bushes, fruit 48

C

cabbages 28-9, **28-9**
  crop rotation 15
  growing times 14
  lime 10
  mini-vegetables 41
  spacing 15

calabrese 29
  growing times 14
  mini-vegetables 41
cardoons **5**, 35, **35**
  division 19
  siting 15
carrot fly 26
carrots 9, 26, 27
  growing in borders 9
  growing times 14
  mini-vegetables 41, **41**
  spacing 15
catch-crops 11, 17, **20**, 21
cauliflowers 28-9, **28**
  growing times 14
  mini-vegetables **40**, 41
celeriac 34, **34**, 35
celery 14, 22, **22**, 23
chard 30, 31
cherries 47
  fan-training **48**, 49
  pruning 49
chervil 51, 55
chicory 21, **21**
Chinese cabbages 30, **30**
chives 50, 54
choy sum 30
clay soils 10, 16
climbing beans, supports **25**
cloches **6**, 11, 59
cold frames 11, **11**, 19, 37, **37**
compost 10, 17
containers 9, 42-3, **42-3**
  greenhouse crops 38
  growing salads in 56
  herbs in 51
cordons 9, 48-9, **49**
corn salad 21
cottage gardens 8
courgettes 33, **33**
  in containers 42
  growing times 14
crop rotation 15, **15**
cucumbers
  in containers 42, 56, 57
  on fences and walls 9
  in greenhouses 38, **38**, 39
  outdoor cucumbers 23, **23**
  seeds 11
cut-and-come-again crops **21**, 57
cuttings 18-19

D

damsons 46-7
designing a kitchen garden 6-7
digging 12-13

dill 55
diseases 11, 15, 58-9
division 19
double digging 12
drainage **12**
draw hoes 12
Dutch hoes 12
dwarf beans 9, **24**, 57

E

endive 21, 22, **22**, 23
espaliers 49, **49**

F

F1 hybrids 11
fan-training **48**, 49
fences, growing crops on 6, 9
fennel, sweet 35
fennel (herb) **52**, 55
fertilizers 11, 16-17
  in containers 43
  mini-vegetables 41
figs 42, **43**
focal points, fruit trees 9
forking soil 13, **13**
forks 12
French beans 14, 25
frost pockets 6
fruit
  in containers 42, 43
  as focal points 9
  propagation 18
  pruning and training 48-9, **48-9**
  soft fruit 44-5, **44-5**
  tree fruits 7, 46-7, **46-7**
fruit cages **10**
fungal diseases 59
fungicides 11, 59

G

gages 46-7
garlic 32, 33
globe artichokes 34, **34**, 35
  division 19
  siting 7, 9, 15
'good king henry' 31
gooseberries 44-5
  in containers 42
  cuttings 19
  pruning and training 48-9
  standards 9
  as windbreaks 6
grand kitchen gardens 8
grape vines 9

green manures 17, **17**
greenhouses **10**, 11, 36-9, **36-9**
growing bags 38, 57

H

hanging baskets 56-7
hardwood cuttings 19
harvesting herbs 51
heating greenhouses 37
hedges, herb 55
herbicides 60
herbs 7, 50-5
  in containers 9, 57
  growing in borders 9
  planning a herb garden 50-1
  propagation 18, 19
hoeing 13, **61**
hoes 12
humus 10, 16
hybrid berries 45
hybrids, F1 11
hyssop 55

I

insecticides 11
insects 58, **58**, **59**
inter-cropping 21

J

Jerusalem artichokes 6, 15, 34, 35

K

kale 9, 30, 31
  growing times 14
  mini-vegetables 41
kohl rabi 14, 41

L

land cress 21
lavender 55
layout 7
leafmould 17
leeks 32-3, **33**
  growing times 14
  mini-vegetables 41
lemon balm 19, **50**, 55
lettuces **8**, 9, 20, **20**, 21
  in containers 42, 43, 57
  growing in borders 9
  growing times 14
  mini-vegetables **40**, 41
  spacing 15

lime 10
liquid manure 16
loganberries 9, 45

M

Malabar spinach 31
manures 10, 16, **16**
  digging in 12-13
marjoram 9, 19, 50, **50**, 51, 52, 53, **53**, 55
marrows **6**, 11, **32**, 33
mini-vegetables 40-1, **40-1**
mint 50, 51, 54-5, **54**
mixed salads 22
mizuna 30
mountain spinach 9, 31
mulches
  organic 17, **17**
  plastic **61**
mushroom compost 16, 17

N

nectarines 47
New Zealand spinach 31, 56
nitrogen 11, 17

O

onions **8**, 32, **32**, 33
  growing times 14
  mini-vegetables 41
  salad onions 20-1
orache 9, 31
organic matter 10, **10**, 16
organic mulches 17, **17**
oriental brassicas 30, 31
ornamental kitchen gardens 8-9, **8-9**
ornamental leaf crops 30

P

pak choi 30
parsley 9, 50, 51, **51**, 53, **53**, 56
parsnips 26, **26**, 27
  mini-vegetables 41
  seeds 11
paths 7, **7**, 57
peaches 47
  in containers 42
  fan-training 49
  pruning 49
pears 9, 46, 47, **47**
  fan-training 49
  pruning and training 9, 48-9, **49**
peas **5**, 9, 14, 24, 25, 57

crop rotation 15
  on fences and walls 9
  growing in borders 9
  growing times 14
  seeds 11
pennyroyal 51, 55
peppers 39, 42
perennial crops 7, 15
pests 8, 11, 15, 58
planning 14-15
planting 10
plums 46-7, 49
pollination, tree fruit 47
polytunnels 36, **36**
potagers 8, **50**
potash 11
potatoes 27, **27**
  in containers 42
  earthing up 27, **27**
  growing times 14
  mini-vegetables 41
propagation 18-19, **18-19**
propagators 37
pruning fruit 48
pumpkins 33, **33**
purslane, summer 21

R

radicchio 9
radishes 14, 20, **20**, 21
raised beds **13**, 57
raspberries 6, 16, 44, **44**, 45
redcurrants 9, 45, **45**
  pruning and training 48-9
rhubarb **5**
  division 19
  growing in borders 9
  siting 7, 15
rocket 23, **23**
root vegetables 26-7, **26-7**
  crop rotation 15
rootstocks, fruit 48
rosemary 9, 51, **52**, 55, **55**
rotation of crops 15, **15**
runner beans 9, 24-5, **24**
  in containers 42, **42**, 57
  growing times 14

S

sage 9, 50, **50**, 51, **52**, 53
'saladini' 22
salads 20-3
  in containers 9, 56
salsify 9, 11, 34-5
sandy soils 10, 16
savory 51, 55

scorzonera 9, 11, 34-5, **35**
seakale beet 15, 31
seed catalogues 11
seedlings, thinning 15
seeds
  sowing 14, 18, **18-19**
  storing 11
  weed seeds 60-1
shade 6
shelter 6
silver chard 31
sloping sites 7
softwood cuttings 18-19
soil
  digging 12-13
  drainage 12, **12**
  fertility 16-17
  forking 13, **13**
  hoeing 13, **61**
  improving 10
sorrel 22, 23
sowing seeds 18, **18-19**
spacing vegetables 14-15
spades 12
spinach **5**, 31, **31**
spinach beet 31
sprouting beans 57
sprouting broccoli **29**
squashes
  in containers 56, 57
  on fences and walls 9
  storing 33
staging, greenhouses 37
standards, fruit 48
'step-over' apples 9, 49
strawberries 43, **43**, 44, **44**, 45
  alpine 9, **42**, 44
  in containers 56, **56**, 57
strawberry towers 43, 57
sunlight 6, 50
supports, climbing beans **25**
sweet peas 6
sweetcorn 6, 9, 56
Swiss chard 9, 31, **31**

T

tarragon 50, **50**, 51, 55
tatsoi 30
thinning seedlings 15
thyme 9, 43, 50, **50**, 51, **52**, 53, **53**, 55
tomatoes
  in containers 42, **42**, 57
  on fences and walls 9
  in greenhouses 38, **38**, 39
  in hanging baskets 56

outdoor tomatoes 23
tools 12
trace elements 17
training
  fruit 48
  greenhouse crops 39, **39**
tunnels 36, **36**
turnips 34, 35
  growing times 14
  mini-vegetables 41
  spacing 15

V

ventilation, greenhouses 36, 37
vines 9
virus diseases 59

W

walls, growing crops on 6, 9
watering 7, 11
  containers 43
  greenhouses 37
weedkillers 61
weeds 11, 60-1, **60-1**
  hoeing 13
  liquid manure 16
white currants 45, **45**
windbreaks 15
window boxes **52**, 57
window sills 57
winds 6
worms 16, 17

63

ACKNOWLEDGMENTS

The producers and authors would like to thank the following for their support in the creation of this book: **Mrs P Mitchell**, **Mrs R Hills** and **Victoria Sanders** for allowing us to photograph in their gardens; **Paul Elding** and **Stuart Watson** at BOURNE VALLEY NURSERIES, Addlestone, Surrey for their advice, materials and studio.

PICTURE CREDITS

KEY: t = top; b = bottom; l = left; r = right; c = centre; D = designer; G = garden

Neil Campbell-Sharp: G: Westwind 24r.

ELSOMS SEEDS LTD: 40r.

GARDEN FOLIO: **Graham Strong** 46r.

John Glover: 10t, 32r, 33br, 38b, 38t, 45r, 48l, 42l, 42r, 43br, 45r, 46bl, 46tr.

HARPUR GARDEN LIBRARY: D: Tessa King-Farlow 8r; Ron Simple 9b.

GARDEN AND WILDLIFE MATTERS PHOTO LIBRARY: 13bl, 16b, 22t, 23b, 31b, 58tr, 59, 60 all, 61tr; **David Cross** 17tl; **John Phipps** 15t, 16b; **Debi Wager** 17r.

Jacqui Hurst: G: Wreatham House 32bl.

Andrew Lawson: G: Barnsley House 6tr, 9t, 31t, 34t, 34b, 37b, 43bl, 45l, 48r, 53c, 54, 55, 59bl.

CLIVE NICHOLS GARDEN PICTURES: **Clive Nichols** G: Ivy Cottage, Dorset 4b; G: Heligan, Hampton Court Show 1998, 5tl; G: Bourton House, Glos 14b; G: Manoir Aux Quat Saisons, Oxon 20b; D: Rupert Golby, Chelsea 1995 29t; G: The Old Rectory, Berks 35b; D: Julie Toll 36t; G: National Asthma, Chelsea 1993 50; 53r; G: The Chef's Roof Garden, Chelsea 1999; D: Sir Terence Conran 56bl; **Graham Strong** 56tl, 57.

PHOTOS HORTICULTURAL PICTURE LIBRARY: 12t, 13t, 17t, 19b, 20t, 22b, 23t, 30b, 35t, 37t, 61bl.

DEREK ST ROMAINE PHOTOGRAPHY: **Derek St Romaine** G: Rosemoor 10l, 10r, 33bl, 38tl, 39r, 53tl, 54tl; D: Matthew Bell & Noula Hancock, Chelsea 1994 52bl, 53l, 54l.

THE GARDEN PICTURE LIBRARY: **David Askham** 28r; **Lynne Brotchie** 52br; **John Glover** 11tr, 32tl, 38tr, 46l, 46r; **Gil Hanly** 27l; **Michael Howes** 28l; **Jacqui Hurst** 21t 32b; **Mayer/Le Scanff** 6l, 26l, 26r, 44bl; **Howard Rice** 29b, 47bl; **Friedrich Strauss** 44br; **Juliette Wade** 6t.

AL TOZER LTD: 40l.

ADDITIONAL PHOTOGRAPHY: **Peter Anderson** 3br, 6b, 11bl, 11bc, 11br, 19ll, 19m, 19tr, 21b, 25br, 33t, 39l, 41b, 43t, 49tl, 49r. **Steve Gorton**, 1, 3tr, 5br, 18 all, 25tl, 25bl, 25bc, 27 all, 32tl, 44tr, 47tr, 49bl, 51t, 52t.

A-Z BOTANICAL **Shelia Orme** G: Dry Stanford Manor, Oxon 51b; **Geoff Kidd** 54b.

Maurice Walker 58bl.

COOL STUFF to SEW

Stephanie Turnbull

W
FRANKLIN WATTS

 An Appleseed Editions book

Paperback edition 2019
First published in 2015 by Franklin Watts

© 2014 Appleseed Editions

Created by Appleseed Editions Ltd,
Well House, Friars Hill, Guestling,
East Sussex TN35 4ET

Designed and illustrated by Guy Callaby
Edited by Mary-Jane Wilkins

ISBN 978-1-4451-4175-6
Dewey Classification: 646.2

A CIP catalogue for this book is available from the British Library.

Picture credits
t = top, b = bottom, l = left, r = right, c = centre
page 1 windu, 2-3 Zhukov Oleg; 4t OtnaYdur, c Elnur;
5c MARGRIT HIRSCH, b Africa Studio; 6tl Lubava, tc tehcheesiong,
b Birute Vijeikiene; 7 Suslik1983; 8t Louella938/all Shutterstock,
b Mim Waller; 9c Liufuyu/Thinkstock, b MARGRIT HIRSCH/
Shutterstock, 10 and 11 Mim Waller; 12l Dancing Fish/Shutterstock,
r Mim Waller; 13 Mim Waller; 14tr Madlen/Shutterstock; c Mim
Waller, b photokup/Shutterstock; 15s and c Mim Waller, b zhu
difeng; 16t Sergey Novikov/both Shutterstock; 17 Mim Waller; 18t
Birute Vijeikiene/Shutterstock, b Mim Waller; 19 Mim Waller; 20
Ljupco Smokovski/Shutterstock; 21 Mim Waller; 22t Shebeko, tl F.
JIMENEZ MECA, b Mim Waller; 23, 24, 25t Mim Waller, b Africa
Studio; 26t Roman Pyshchyk/both Shutterstock, b Mim Waller;
27t Mim Waller, b kuleczka; 28t keantian/both Shutterstock, r
Mim Waller, b Chimpinski; 29t mark higgins/Shutterstock, b Mim
Waller; 30t LooksLikeLisa, b Birute Vijeikiene; 31 SisterF/all
Shutterstock lightbulb in Cool Ideas boxes Designs Stock/
Shutterstock
Cover Jupiterimages/Thinkstock

Printed in China

Franklin Watts
An imprint of Hachette Children's Group
Part of The Watts Publishing Group
Carmelite House
50 Victoria Embankment
London EC4Y 0DZ

An Hachette UK Company
www.hachette.co.uk

www.franklinwatts.co.uk

Contents

4   Start sewing!

6   Needles and thread

8   Simple stitches

10 Fantastic felt

12 Cool creatures

14 Buttons and beads

16 Sock puppets

18 Brilliant bags

20 Clothes craft

22 Bath-time treats

24 Get decorating!

26 Clever cards

28 Amazing art

30 Glossary

31 Websites

32 Index

Start sewing!

Sewing is a really cool craft. It's not expensive or difficult to do, and with just a few easy stitches and some basic materials you can create fantastic games, toys, bags, cards and much more.

Good sewing kits include all kinds of useful items, such as scissors, pins, needles, buttons and thread.

Did You Know?

The skill of sewing by hand goes back to prehistoric times, when people made fur and skin clothes using bone needles and thread from stringy animal sinews.

Hand sewing

Sewing machines are great time-saving devices for putting together complicated clothes, but it's best to learn to hand sew first. None of the projects in this book needs a sewing machine – just a needle, thread and some fabric.

Clever crafts

Sewing is handy for everyday tasks such as mending clothes, but it can also be amazingly creative. Skilled artists sew intricate **embroideries**, **tapestries** and patchwork quilts or wall hangings. Other sewing experts design and produce unique hand-made shoes, hats and furniture.

Quilters sew shaped pieces of fabric together, then stitch on thick backing layers of fabric.

Cool Idea

Sewing equipment is small and easy to lose, so keep needles in cases and pins in pin cushions. Store thread neatly in a tin or box so it doesn't get in a tangle!

Start with the simple projects in this book and who knows – one day you might be a famous fashion designer, craft expert or artist!

Needles and thread

The first step in learning to sew is to find a needle! Ordinary sewing needles are straight, sharp-ended and vary in size according to the thickness of your thread and fabric.

Steady threading

Cut a length of thread: not so short that you can only sew a few stitches, but not so long that it gets tangled. A piece the length of your arm is about right. Feed it through the needle's eye (hole) and tie a knot. Sit in a well-lit place so you can see what you're doing.

1. Snip the top of the thread at an angle to make a neat point. It's hard to push a ragged end through the eye. Or you could wet it in your mouth to create a flatter tip.

2. Hold the needle between your thumb and first finger, with the eye facing you. Pick up the end of the thread with your other thumb and first finger and feed it through the eye.

Cool Idea

*If you have a sewing kit, it may include a **threader**. Push the wire loop through the needle's eye, feed the thread through the loop, then pull it back through the eye. Hey presto – a threaded needle!*

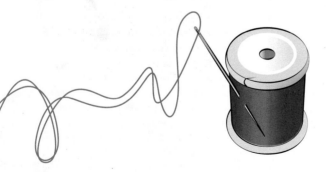

3. Pull at least 15 cm of thread through the eye, otherwise it may fall out again. Now stick the needle safely into a pin cushion or cotton reel while you tie the knot at the end of the thread.

4. *Take the end in one hand and use your free hand to wrap it once around your first finger. Hold it in place with your thumb.*

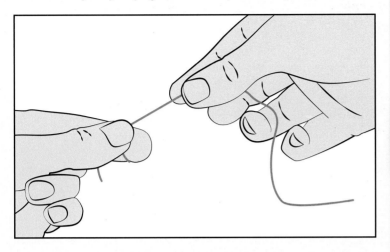

5. *Use your thumb to roll the loop slowly off your finger...*

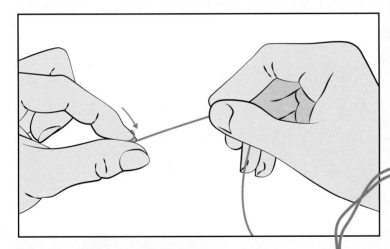

6. *...then trap it and push it back with the tip of your middle finger, so it forms a knot.*

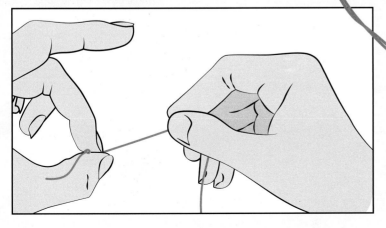

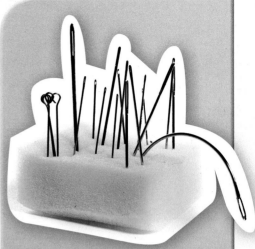

Did You Know?

Embroidery needles have an extra-long eye for thick thread. **Darning** *needles are fat and blunt for pushing through thick material, and some needles are curved for reaching awkward angles.*

Single or double?

Sewing with a single thread is good when you want stitches to be thin and hidden. If you go wrong, it's easy to unthread the needle, unpick stitches, then thread it again.

For thicker, stronger stitches, use a double thread. This means pulling the thread further in step 3, then looping and rolling both ends together in steps 4 and 5.

Simple stitches

You only need a few stitches to start with. Follow these easy steps to learn three basic (but very useful) stitches. Find a scrap of fabric to practise them on, making sure not to pull the stitches too tight.

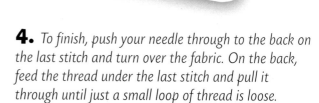

Running stitch

This is probably the easiest stitch of all.

1. *Push your needle up through the fabric, so the knot is on the back. Now push the needle back through, and up again, in the line where you want to stitch.*

2. *Pull the needle through so the thread is tight. You've made your first stitch!*

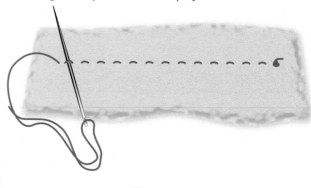

3. *Carry on in the same way to the end of the line. Try to keep the stitches the same size.*

4. *To finish, push your needle through to the back on the last stitch and turn over the fabric. On the back, feed the thread under the last stitch and pull it through until just a small loop of thread is loose.*

5. *Feed the needle through the loop and pull it tight to make a knot. Cut off the thread.*

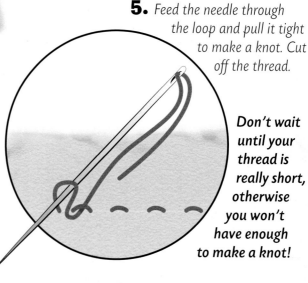

Don't wait until your thread is really short, otherwise you won't have enough to make a knot!

Cool Idea

Try lacing a contrasting colour thread in and out of running stitches to make a wiggly effect.

Backstitch

Backstitch is like running stitch, but you keep going back to fill in gaps between stitches. It creates a neat, unbroken line. Start with steps 1 and 2 of running stitch, then poke the needle back through the fabric at the end of the first stitch.

Push the needle back up a space away from the stitch, then pull through the thread. Repeat to fill the line.

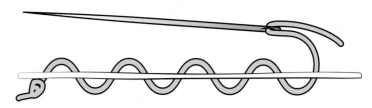

Running stitch runs up and down through the material like this...

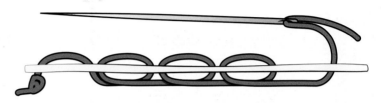

... but backstitch loops back each time like this.

Up-and-over stitch

To sew two pieces of fabric together, start by pushing the needle up through the top layer of fabric, so the knot will be hidden in the middle.

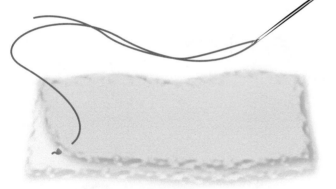

Then feed the needle and thread up from the bottom layer, out of the top layer, then back round to the bottom layer again. Repeat all the way along.

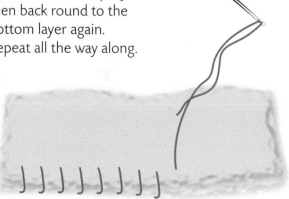

Did You Know?

Cross-stitch is a traditional style of sewing that has been used for hundreds of years to embroider patterns and pictures.

Fantastic felt

Felt is the perfect fabric for sewing. It comes in bright colours, is easy to cut and doesn't fray. Here are two cool felt craft projects to try. They're ideal for practising the three types of stitches from pages 8 and 9.

Tic tac toe

This fun felt board game is really quick and easy to make. Why not give it to someone as a gift?

1. *Cut a 15 cm square of felt in any colour. Using a ruler and pins, mark two vertical lines and two horizontal lines, each 5 cm apart.*

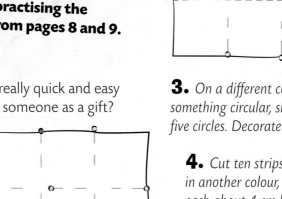

2. *Sew along each line in brightly-coloured thread, removing each pin as you come to it.*

3. *On a different coloured felt piece, draw round something circular, such as a bottle top, and cut out five circles. Decorate them with stitching if you like.*

4. *Cut ten strips in another colour, each about 4 cm long. Sew them in pairs to make five crosses.*

Enjoy your game of tic tac toe!

Handy holders

Try stitching felt pockets to create a useful wall hanger for storing all your bits and bobs.

1. *Find or cut some rectangles of colourful felt.*

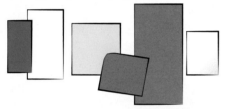

2. *Fold up a rectangle to leave a flap at the top, like this, and pin it in place.*

3. *Choose a bright thread that stands out against the felt, then sew up the two sides to make a pocket. Use running stitch, backstitch or up-and-over stitch.*

Thick, doubled thread stands out better.

4. *When you've made a few pockets, fix them to a cork board with drawing pins.*

Add stitches on the front of the pockets for decoration.

Cool Idea

Cover your cork board in fabric first to make it even more colourful. A pillowcase wrapped tightly around the board and taped at the back works well.

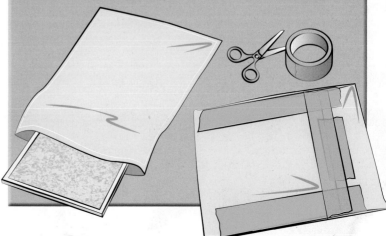

Cool creatures

Once you've tried sewing with felt, you can cut more complicated shapes and create amazing animal toys. Experiment with the designs on this page, then invent more of your own!

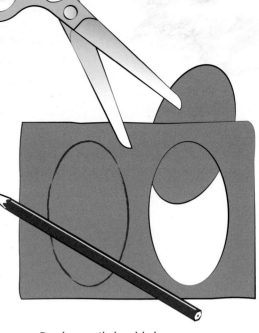

Body basics

To make animal characters, you first need a body template. Draw an oval, about 8 cm long, on paper or card and cut it out.

Draw around your template twice on to felt. Try starting with brown felt to make a bear. Cut out the shapes.

Dark pencil should show up, or use ballpoint pen – but then turn the felt piece over, so pen marks are on the back.

Cut small shapes for ears and four paws, plus a circle of white felt for the bear's muzzle.

Did You Know?

The art of decorating fabric using stitches and other, smaller pieces of fabric or decorations is called appliqué.

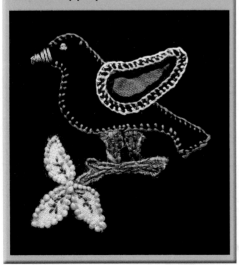

Start sewing

Now make up your bear!

1. *First, sew the white muzzle on to one of the body ovals with small, neat running stitches in white thread.*

2. *Using a doubled black thread, make lots of little stitches to create eyes and a nose. Make a mouth with backstitch.*

3. Put the two body ovals together and sew along the edges with brown running stitch. When you come to places where an ear or paw should go, sandwich them between the ovals and stitch them, too.

Don't go all the way round – leave a gap.

4. Use your fingertips to gently push a little cotton wool inside to pad out your bear.

5. Finally, finish sewing round the edge.

More ideas

Now make more animals, using the same basic design: two body ovals plus extra paws, legs, tails or wings! Remember to stitch details on the face or body before sewing the ovals together. Soon you could have a whole zoo of furry animals...

Cool Idea

Turn felt animals into finger puppets by keeping the base unstitched and leaving out the stuffing. Unstuffed animals also make great bookmarks.

The creatures you make may depend on the colours of felt you have.

Buttons and beads

Why not attach other decorations to fabric, such as buttons and beads? They're easy to sew on with just a few stitches, as long as your needle is thin enough to go through the holes.

Button badges

Make arty badges by layering different coloured felt shapes, then adding a bright button on top. Sew it all together with thick thread in an 'x' through the button holes. Sew a small strip of felt to the back with a safety pin in the middle and your badge is ready.

Make sure the safety pin is positioned to open outwards so you can pin it on.

Cool Idea

Look in charity shops for clothes with interesting or unusual buttons. They may be a lot cheaper than buying a new set of buttons.

Most buttons are plastic, but some are made of metal, wood or shell. Instead of holes, some have a moulded loop on the back called a shank.

Cool key rings

Make a personalized key ring using a plain metal key ring, felt, thread and extra decorations. Choose buttons or beads to design funny faces, patterns or your initials.

1. Draw around a circular object, such as a cookie cutter, on felt. Draw another circle about 3 cm beneath, and draw lines to connect the two, like this.

These go back to back to make up the two halves of your key ring.

2. Cut out the shape and decorate each circle. The section of circle connected to the central strip will be the top of each.

3. Feed one felt circle through a metal key ring. Sew the circles together with an up-and-over stitch. Add a little cotton wool padding before sewing the last bit.

Use a double thread and sew on each bead with several stitches to make sure it's firmly fixed.

Did You Know?

Traditional Chinese buttons are made of knotted strings and are called frogs.

Bling a bag

You can sew decorations directly on to clothes or other fabrics. Why not find a plain canvas bag, cover it in bright buttons, beads and thin strips of ribbon, then give it to your mum or gran as a gift?

Sock puppets

Sock puppets are fun to make, and they look better and last longer if they're sewn rather than held together with glue. Find a few old, clean socks and some spare buttons then design a cast of crazy characters.

Funny faces

1. *Put your sock on a hand, heel on top, and mark pen dots where you want the eyes to go.*

2. *Sew on two large buttons, tying the thread inside the sock. You may need to roll up the open end to reach inside.*

3. *Cut a red felt oval to sew underneath the toe end of the sock and make your character's mouth. Add a pink tongue.*

4. *Sew two small beads to the tip of the toe for nostrils.*

Animal ears

There are several ways of making animal ears. One method is to sew on two pieces of felt to make long, floppy dog ears, like this.

Instead try turning the sock inside out and snip the heel down the middle.

Adding extras

Now add more features to give your puppet personality!

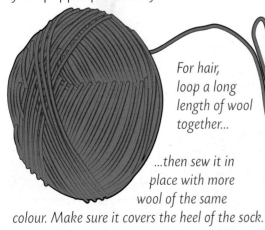

For hair, loop a long length of wool together...

...then sew it in place with more wool of the same colour. Make sure it covers the heel of the sock.

Add glasses made from a pipe cleaner, jewellery from beads threaded on elastic or sew on a bow tie, scarf or hair ribbon. Use your imagination!

Use an up-and-over stitch to sew the cut edges together. Turn the sock the right way out and two little ears will poke up. Stuff them with cotton wool to make them stand up well.

Cool Idea
Take funny photos of your sock puppets and send them to friends to make them smile.

It's easy to unpick stitching and remove or adjust features that aren't in quite the right place. Don't stop until you're happy with your creation!

Did You Know?

A wrestler named Mick Foley wore a sock puppet on his hand during fights and used it to perform wrestling moves on his opponents!

Brilliant bags

Drawstring bags are great sewing projects. They're also useful for storing your stuff, whether you need a secret container for precious things or a spacious tote bag to cart around your swimming kit!

Speedy felt bag

Use this soft bag as a money pouch, or give it away as a smart gift bag. You can vary the size to make a bigger or taller bag.

1. *Cut a rectangle of felt and fold it double.*

2. *Sew up each long side. Use backstitch to hold the **seams** together firmly.*

3. *Turn the bag inside out. Use thick thread to sew large running stitches around the bag, near the top. Start at the front, and don't pull the thread all the way through.*

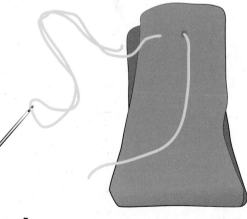

4. *Remove the needle and cut the two dangling ends of thread to the same length. Pull to tighten them and tie in a bow.*

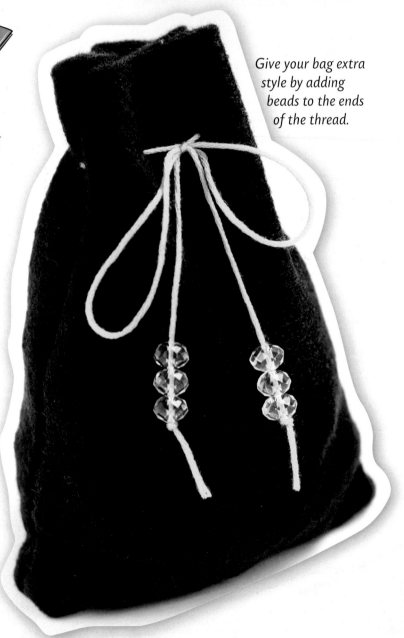

Give your bag extra style by adding beads to the ends of the thread.

Pillow bags

Pillowcases are practically bags already – all you need to do is add a drawstring. Here's how.

1. *Find an old pillowcase and turn it inside out.*

2. *Use small, sharp scissors (or a **seam ripper**) to snip the stitches from the top of a side seam. Stop when you've made a 5 cm split.*

5 cm

Don't snip the fabric!

3. *Fold down the top of the pillowcase 2.5 cm, level with the end of the split. Pin in place.*

One side will be double thickness because of the inner flap.

4. *Stitch all the way round the pillowcase with small, neat running stitches. This creates a tube (called a casing) for the drawstring to go through.*

This will be the inside of your bag, so make sure you tie knots on this side.

5. *Turn the pillowcase right side out. Find a long piece of cord, string, ribbon or plaited wool. Attach a large safety pin to the end and feed it through the casing.*

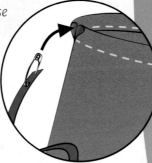

6. *Remove the safety pin. Your drawstring bag is ready to fill!*

Cool Idea

Choose a patterned pillowcase, or add lines of stitching, buttons or beads to liven up a plain one.

Clothes craft

You can transform more than just pillowcases. Here are some great ways of recycling your old clothes into cool stuff for your bedroom.

Have a clear out and find stuff you don't wear!

Clever cushions

If you have a pile of T-shirts you've outgrown but still love, turn them into cushions. It's a cool way of making your bed or chairs more comfortable, and it brightens up your room, too.

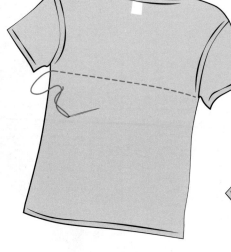

1. *Turn a T-shirt inside out and sew across the chest, just below the arms, using backstitch. You can mark out a straight line with pins first to guide you.*

2. *Cut away the top of the T-shirt, about 1 cm above the sewn line.*

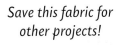

Save this fabric for other projects!

3. *Turn the T-shirt right side out and fill it with pillow stuffing, cotton wool, old towels or socks.*

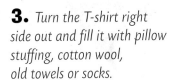

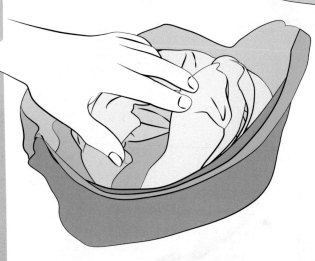

4. *Stitch up the opening. Go along the seams so your stitches don't show.*

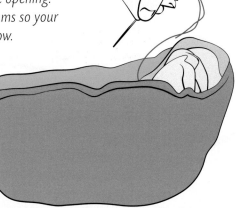

Keep your T-shirt cushion simple, like this one, or sew on buttons and other decorations.

Secret sewing

Do you need a place to hide secret notes, keys or pocket money from nosy brothers or sisters? Find something you don't wear any more – preferably with an inner lining – then sew a felt pocket to the lining. The stitches won't show and no one will know the pocket is there!

Cool Idea

Make a felt pocket like those on page 11 and sew the flap around a coat hanger. Cover it with clothes and you have a secret compartment!

Did You Know?

You can buy socks and even underwear with secret zip compartments for storing valuables!

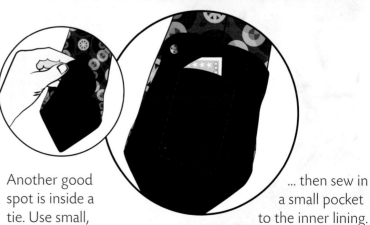

Another good spot is inside a tie. Use small, sharp scissors to unpick the seam a little way...

... then sew in a small pocket to the inner lining. Sew a small **press stud fastener** to each side of the tie seam to close it – so no one will see it's not sewn.

21

Bath-time treats

Terry cloth is a soft, woven fabric used for making towels and wash cloths. It's ideal for sewing this hooded towel and matching mitt. They make great gifts for your friends and family – or keep them for yourself!

Cosy hoodie

To make this easy hooded towel you need one big bath towel and one hand towel.

1. Cut the hand towel in half. Put one half aside for making the bath mitt later.

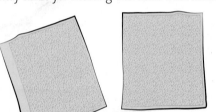

2. Lay the bath towel on the floor, underside up. Position half of the hand towel at the top, in the middle, also with the underside facing up. Pin the edges together.

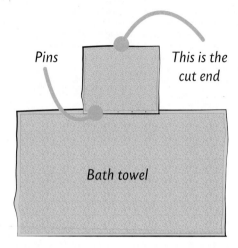

Pins

This is the cut end

Bath towel

3. Stitch the edges together using backstitch.

4. Turn over the towels, then fold them in half, like this. Pin the cut end of the hand towel together about 3 cm from the top and sew it up with backstitch.

Pin and sew this edge 3 cm from the top.

5. Turn your hood the right way out and your towel is finished!

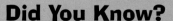

Did You Know?

The world's most expensive bath towels are made from soft, plush Egyptian cotton and cost about £800 each!

*Decorate your mitt by sewing colourful ribbon or **rickrack** neatly around it.*

Easy mitt

Making a bath mitt with the other half of the hand towel is even simpler.

1. *Make a template. Sketch a round-ended rectangle on scrap paper, like this. It should be bigger than your hand (or the hand of the person who'll be using the mitt).*

2. *Cut out the template and pin it on the towel, lining up the bottom edges.*

3. *Cut around the template, leaving at least 1 cm extra all the way round.*

4. *Make a second mitt shape in the same way and pin the two together, about 1 cm from the edge. Check the undersides of the towel shapes are facing outwards.*

5. *Sew the shapes together and remove all the pins. Turn your finished mitt the right way out.*

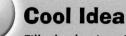

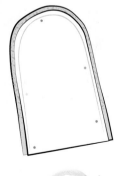

Cool Idea

Fill a bath mitt with fancy soaps to make a really thoughtful gift for someone special.

Get decorating!

It's easy to sew great decorations for parties and celebrations. Why not adapt the animal designs from pages 12 and 13 to make Easter eggs, Halloween pumpkins or Christmas gingerbread men? Here are some more decoration ideas.

Great garlands

Make simple garlands from felt shapes and hang them from curtain rails and lampshades, or loop them around the room in long strings.

1. *Decide on a shape and cut out card templates. Circles, stars and diamonds work well. Draw around the templates on felt and cut out the shapes.*

2. *Lay the shapes in a line and sew them together with running stitch. Don't pull the thread all the way through – leave a long tail at each end for hanging your garland.*

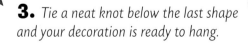

3. *Tie a neat knot below the last shape and your decoration is ready to hang.*

Cool Idea

Sew layers of felt shapes together and thread small craft pompoms in between to make your garlands really eye-catching.

Fun flags

Strings of flags called bunting are perfect for indoor or outdoor parties, or just for brightening up your bedroom. Make them using old shirts, sheets or scraps of patterned fabric.

1. *Draw a triangle template on card. Add a flap at the top and cut it out.*

Draw around the template on the underside of the material, so the pen marks won't show.

2. *Cut triangles from your material using the template.*

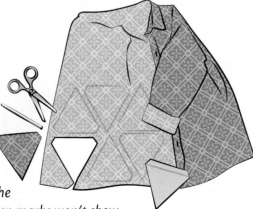

3. *Fold the flap of each triangle over a long strip of thin ribbon, pin them in place, then sew along the ribbon with running stitch.*

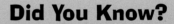

Go through both layers of fabric so it's firmly fixed.

4. *Leave some ribbon at each end for tying or taping up your bunting.*

Clever cards

Use your sewing skills to create special home-made cards. Stitch patterns on felt, then stick the fabric on colourful card using **PVA glue**. Or forget the fabric altogether and sew directly on to card!

Prick and stitch

Use this prick and stitch method for sewing on card. Don't make the holes too close together, or the card may tear.

1. Draw a simple picture, pattern or letter on the back of a piece of card.

2. Rest the card on an old notepad or pile of magazines. Use a thick, blunt darning needle to prick evenly-spaced holes round the shape. Press hard.

The holes don't need to go all the way through the card. They will show up as bumps on the other side.

3. Turn over the card and sew around your shape, using the bumps to guide your needle. Work slowly and carefully to avoid bending or tearing the card.

Cool Idea

For unique party invitations or gift tags, make holes with a hole punch around rectangles of card, then thread ribbon in and out of the holes.

As you finish each colour, cut the thread at the back and tape down the end.

4. Cut out your finished design and **mount** it on a large piece of folded card.

Thread a few small beads on to stitches to add extra texture.

Starbursts

Now try this really cool card-sewing trick.

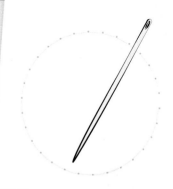

1. Draw a circle on card and prick holes around it. Make sure there are an even number of holes.

2. Turn over the card. Pull thread up through one hole and down the hole directly opposite. Count the holes on either side to check it's the right hole.

Use a long piece of thread.

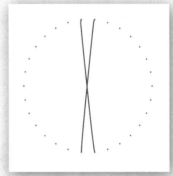

3. Come up at the hole to the left of the one you just went down, and take the thread across the circle again, going down at the hole on the right of the first.

4. Keep going like this until you've been through each hole. Cut the thread at the back and tape down the end.

Make lots of similar shapes to create a fantastic starburst pattern.

Did You Know?

*Many **scrapbook** makers use thread to stitch fancy borders around pages or sew on fabric decorations called embellishments.*

Amazing art

Don't throw away scraps of fabric, extra buttons, bits of thread and odd lengths of ribbon. Keep them in a big box or tin and use them to create fantastic pieces of art.

Ribbon stripes

Here's an easy idea to start with. Find a photo frame and cut a piece of felt to fit inside it. Arrange strips of ribbon across the felt in a criss-cross pattern.

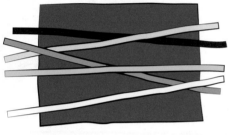

Use a plain frame in a contrasting colour to make your pattern stand out.

Take a photo of the strips so you remember the arrangement, then move them off the felt. Sew them on, one by one, using running stitch. Choose thread that matches each ribbon and make the stitches on the top very small, so they're not obvious.

Frame your stripy picture and display it!

Cool Idea

Ask an adult to iron any ribbons or scraps of material before you use them. They'll lie flatter on the felt and be easier to sew.

Cool collages

A great way of using up leftovers is to create a big, sewn **collage**. Look at the colours and textures of your fabric scraps to give you ideas, then sketch out a scene on paper.

Don't make your design too complicated. You can always add extra details later.

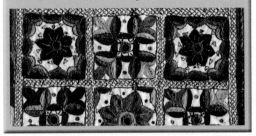
Start with a big piece of felt for the background, then sew on smaller pieces of fabric to build up the picture. Use layers to create depth and add ribbon, lace, buttons and beads for fine details. You could even sew on extras such as feathers, plastic gems and sequins.

Glossary

collage
A collection of materials, artistically arranged and fixed in place, either by sewing or gluing.

cross-stitch
A type of embroidery in which blocks of many small 'x'-shaped stitches build up pictures and patterns.

darning
A method of mending holes or worn areas, for example in socks, by weaving thread in and out of the fabric.

embroidery
The craft of decorating fabric using different stitches made with a needle and thread.

felt
Fabric made from pressed, matted wool.

fray
To unravel into loose threads at the edges.

mount
To fix something in place on a background to display it.

pinking shears
Scissors with blades that are serrated, like a saw.

press stud fastener
A pair of small metal or plastic discs that snap together and pull apart.

rickrack

PVA glue
A strong, water-based glue, also known as white craft glue. PVA stands for polyvinyl acetate, which is a rubbery plastic substance.

rickrack
Flat, narrow, cotton braid, woven in a wavy, zigzag shape.

scrapbook
A decorated album that may be filled with photos, drawings, notes and other personal details or keepsakes.

seam
The join where two pieces of fabric have been sewn together.

seam ripper
A small tool with a forked handle, used for lifting and cutting through stitches to unpick them.

tapestry
A woven piece of art using two sets of interlaced threads. The threads are held in place on a device called a loom.

threader
A small device for helping to thread a needle. Threaders are usually made of thin, flimsy metal, so use them carefully.

seam ripper

Websites

www.holiday-crafts-and-creations.com/craft-tips.html
Find clear instructions and photos to help you learn basic stitches.

www.thecraftycrow.net/sewing-stitchery
Discover all kinds of simple sewing projects for beginners.

www.activityvillage.co.uk/felt-crafts
Practise your sewing skills with these fun felt crafts.

www.thesewingdirectory.co.uk/projects-for-children
Lots of ideas for simple projects that children and adults can work on together.

Index

animal characters 12, 13, 16
appliqué 12

backstitch 9, 11, 12, 18, 20,
  22
badges 14
bags 4, 15, 18, 19
ballpoint pens 12
bath mitt 22, 23
beads 14, 15, 16, 18, 19,
  26, 29
bookmarks 13
bunting 25
button badges 14
buttons 4, 14, 15, 16, 19, 21,
  28, 29

cards 4, 26, 27
clothes 4, 5, 15, 20, 21
collages 29, 30
cord 19
cork boards 11
cotton reels 6
cotton wool 13, 15, 16, 20
cross-stitch 9, 30
cushions 20, 21, 29

darning 7, 30
decorations 24, 25
double thread 7, 11, 12, 15

embroidery 5, 7, 9, 30

fabric 4, 5, 6, 8, 9, 10, 11, 12,
  15, 20, 25, 26, 28, 29
feathers 29

felt 10, 11, 12, 13, 14, 15, 16,
  18, 21, 24, 26, 28, 29, 30
flags 25
fraying 10, 25, 30

games 4, 10
garlands 24
gems 29
gifts 10, 15, 18, 22, 23
gift tags 26

key rings 15
knots 6, 7, 8, 9, 19, 24

lace 29

mats 29
mending 5

needles 4, 5, 6, 7, 8, 9, 14,
  18, 26

party invitations 26
patchwork quilts 5, 29
pencils 12
pillowcases 11, 19, 20
pin cushions 5, 6
pinking shears 25, 30
pins 4, 5, 10, 11, 19, 20, 22, 23
pipe cleaners 16
pockets 11, 21
pompoms 24
pouches 18
press stud fasteners 21, 30
prick and stitch 26, 27
PVA glue 26, 30

quilting 5, 29

ribbon 15, 19, 23, 25, 26,
  28, 29
rickrack 23, 30
running stitch 8, 9, 11, 12,
  13, 18, 19, 24, 25, 28

safety pins 14, 19
scissors 4, 19, 21, 25
seam ripper 19, 30
seams 18, 19, 20, 21, 30
sequins 29
sewing kits 4, 6
sewing machines 4
sock puppets 16, 17
stitches 4, 7, 8, 9, 12, 13, 15,
  16, 18, 19, 20, 21, 22, 26, 28
string 19
stuffing 13, 16, 20

tapestries 5, 30
terry cloth 22
thread 4, 5, 6, 7, 8, 9, 10, 11, 14,
  15, 18, 24, 26, 27, 28
threader 6, 30
tic tac toe 10
towels 20, 22, 23
toys 4, 12
T-shirts 20, 21

up-and-over stitch 9, 11, 15, 16

wall hangings 5, 11
wash cloths 22
wool 11, 16, 19

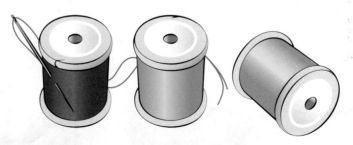